BECOME YOUR OWN
BIPOLAR LIFE COACH

by

Wendy Lavin

**Grosvenor House
Publishing Limited**

Wendy Lavin is hereby identified as author of this
work in accordance with Section 77 of the Copyright, Designs
and Patents Act 1988

The book cover picture is copyright to Wendy Lavin

This book is published by
Grosvenor House Publishing Ltd
28-30 High Street, Guildford, Surrey, GU1 3EL.
www.grosvenorhousepublishing.co.uk

A CIP record for this book
is available from the British Library

ISBN 978-1-78148-778-5

Dedication

*To Ste, my soul mate, my best friend;
my hero. For all that you are and for
all that you do ... with gratitude.*

About the Author

Wendy Lavin was finally diagnosed with bipolar disorder in 2002, following many years of unexplained highs, depressions and madness. She has spent many years learning about and managing her condition. She has been involved in supporting mental health work and charities and has taken part in research into bipolar disorder and its causes.

Wendy is a life coach and founder of Lavin Coaching Associates Limited. She has spent a number of years working as a qualified advice and guidance practitioner. She lives in Merseyside, UK with her beloved husband.

Contents

"What progress, you ask, have I made? I have begun to be a friend to myself."

Hecato, Greek philosopher.

Introduction

When you have spectacularly cheated on your partner, overspent and realised that you have not been yourself despite, at the time, feeling more like yourself than ever before, and when you have felt so close to having the answer to life's big questions and you can live your life in an elevated magnificence before descending into a black abyss, you may have bipolar disorder.

I look back now and see distorted images of a girl flying high; of soaring confidence in a world so open in possibilities that the light and glory could blind you. With the pressured speech needed to get my many thoughts and insights out into the world, I thought I was great company and, when things were not too high, I probably was. I was the epitome of 'the life and soul of the party' – funny as hell and flirty. But when I was too high, I could be so endlessly creative, angry and frustrated that other mere mortals could not keep up with my thoughts and ideas.

I could go from the party girl to another level of risk-taking behaviour, causing chaos and hurt. This was mania, and for me the mania comes first, followed by what can only be described as a living hell – an inner world so painful; so black, so tortured that even now to think of it, I feel fear and a desperate desire to never enter that inner world again. This is depression. For me, this comes second, like God's punishment for daring to feel unadulterated joy and unrealistic confidence and for unwittingly causing chaos and hurt. In the depths of depression, my tortured mind almost enjoys the pain because I deserve it – because I am the most useless, worthless human being that has ever walked the earth.

I have tried over the years to describe to other people the depressions I have experienced, and each time I have come up short. I cannot explain it. All I can say is that it is black; it is deep, it destroys you from the inside out and it shows no mercy. Add to this the psychosis: a paranoid world where people are out to get you. A world in which you relive traumatic events from the past, where some of the worst messages you were given in childhood repeat themselves on automatic loop, which is only right, because you deserve this torture. I have come across people who say they are depressed because they have had a bad experience, and this can be termed as depression. They may sit and cry and lose some interest in life's pleasures, but when I have seen people like this, I have felt jealous. In my depressions, there is no point in crying or in anything, as all there is and can ever be is a terrifying darkness.

It is commonly thought that only cowards commit suicide, and in some cases, this may be true. But I know that unless you have experienced a depression so deep, so painful and so relentless, you cannot begin to understand how suicide may be the only option. You are not aware of the pain you may cause the survivors, because only you know how happy they will be when you are gone. Many times, I have longed for death – a death with no afterlife, because in this, there is the promise of silence; of nothingness and of peace.

I think back to a 23-year-old young woman who had just gained a degree, was full of life and promise and who lay on her bedroom floor in the early hours of the morning, having not washed, eaten or slept for several days, and who was trying to summon the energy and guts to drive a knife through her chest.

That sums up my early experiences of bipolar disorder: fantastic and life-affirming highs, followed by crippling lows. Weeks and months spent in psychiatric institutions on 24-hour watch, where your bags are searched, where you are fed medication, where your mood is monitored and where you are scary and scared. Psychiatric institutions where you meet staff who don't understand, who don't even know if they 'believe' what you say and where you also meet staff who are so committed, so insightful, so tender and so caring, it would renew your faith in mankind. The different ends of the scales in care have been striking.

To finally be diagnosed with bipolar disorder (also known as manic depression) feels like a life sentence, yet it brings with it a relief that there is a name for this and more importantly, there are treatments. There is recognition that this is something medical and you are not mad, insane or subhuman. However, there is no cure for this condition and research is still in its infancy. On a positive note, I have been diagnosed in a time where there are options and where there is more enlightenment: times in which the *Disability Discrimination Act* protects my employment rights and access to services; times in which medication can be taken orally at home, times in which the options available are not confined to a life in an institution, electric shock therapy or being hidden away from society. For this, I am wholeheartedly grateful.

That is not to say that medicine is a complete or easy fix, or that I have not faced stigma and ignorance. Loved ones have often not been able to hide their disappointment that I have this condition and have taken a long time to accept it, if they truly have at all. My life has been full of people who offer advice and think I am weak for taking medication, time out or whatever it has been that I needed to do.

Old school thinking is that we do not talk about our problems, and sadly, England is the home of the stiff upper lip. If you just get on with it and don't speak of emotions, it is implied that you are strong; that you are a more worthy and fully functioning member of society. To me, this is a lie. We are all the same: we need food to live; oxygen to live, and money to live, but to truly live – to truly know what it is to be here, to be alive and to be present, we need to feel. We need an emotional life and a healthy inner life.

Psychiatric services in this country do their best. I have been under the care of some dedicated and brilliant psychiatrists and supported by some caring nursing staff. They have cared for me when I could not care for myself.

They have medicated me when I was flying high and sat with me on 24-hour watch when I have wanted nothing more than to die. But sadly, like many areas of care, time is limited for patients, and there are budget constraints. As a result, I made a decision a number of years ago to do all I could to stay well, to counsel myself, to educate myself, to truly look at my inner life and most of all, to stay positive and work with the hand I had been dealt; in short, to be my own bipolar life coach.

I have read some inspirational books and publications that have provided me with knowledge and reassurance. I wanted to contribute to the support given to people with bipolar disorder and decided to write an open, honest and practical book for people living with bipolar, written by someone who knows what it is like. I do not profess to be a medical expert or an authority on this condition, but what I can offer is insight, experience and positive, practical tips on living with and managing this condition and making the most of this precious and beautiful thing called life.

For a number of years, I have worked as an advice and guidance practitioner and developed well in my career. I realised that there could be another level to this area of work and subsequently trained as a life coach. My practice in this area has been rewarding beyond compare, and this book builds on that experience of motivating, supporting and empowering people. What it hopefully provides is a positive message to those dealing with the curve balls that living with bipolar disorder can throw. Be assured that I still stumble and experience episodes. This book is not a cure-all, but it is a message of practical hope from someone who decided long ago not to be a victim; someone who took positive action to make meaningful changes to her life, her emotional well-being and more importantly, her outlook.

Mania is not the true me; deep depression is not the true me – but sometimes I wonder what is the true me? I am a mass of contradictions, as are most people with bipolar disorder, and all we can do is make the best of it. A few years ago, Stephen Fry[1] took part in an honest and moving documentary on bipolar disorder. Many of the people he spoke to said that if given the chance to push a button and be rid of the condition forever, they would not push it. I am on the fence. On the days when I feel overwhelmed by its enormity or an episode is coming, I feel I would push the button and push it hard. However, on more philosophical days, I wonder if I would.

If it were not for this condition, would I know myself as well as I do? Would I feel such joy in the good times because I have felt such pain? Would I be able to support people in a genuine way? One of my heroines is Kay Redfield Jamison[2], a Professor of Psychiatry and writer with bipolar disorder who, despite its many drawbacks, has managed to appreciate her condition and see its positives and its beauty. It has taken me a long time, and there are days when I have beaten my fists against the wall in anger at my condition and the restrictions it can impose, but yes, to be honest, I do see a complex beauty in the experiences it has given me.

If you have bipolar disorder, I hope you find the book useful in a practical and positive way, and that you learn to live with your condition the best you can. I wish you luck, love and light.

If you have a loved one with bipolar disorder, I urge you to read on.

If you are a mental health professional, I hope this is of interest for your practice.

Wendy.

CHAPTER ONE

Diagnosis

Straight away, I will point out that I am not a doctor, psychiatrist or physician for the mentally ill in any way. My experience is limited to my personal journey with bipolar disorder and my work as a life coach. Therefore, if you think you may need a diagnosis or are questioning one, seek the help of the medical professionals.

Before my diagnosis, I did a lot of research into what these experiences could be. It was not until my third stay in a psychiatric ward that I was finally and correctly diagnosed with bipolar disorder. Why did it take three times? My response to this would not be to criticise medical practitioners, although at the time I did – why could they not see what was going on? To many, the mania is normal. Why would one not want to experience this feeling of euphoria? It is akin to saying, 'I don't want to be happy'. Therefore, many people present at psychiatric services when they are experiencing low mood. The despair, the psychosis, the bleak nothingness is tangible and can be a reason for treatment, as opposed to, 'I feel great…I need medical help'. The down side of this is that I was being prescribed the wrong levels of medication for almost two years, as I was treated for depression and not bipolar disorder, and this may have contributed to more manic phases.

Over the years, my behaviour has, in hindsight, been strange and larger than life. I think if people had suggested there was something wrong at the time, I would have denied it. I didn't really know much about bipolar disorder and I certainly would not have identified with it. Some of my first highs were at university – but were we not supposed to be living these years of freedom and discovery with gay abandon? Looking back, I probably went a bit far. The depressions that followed were more led by anxiety than deep depression and I, like many, self-medicated with alcohol. Again, excessive drinking is a staple of university life and so was not questioned. It was only during my third stay in hospital that a psychiatrist, to whom I probably owe my life, correctly diagnosed me as having bipolar disorder. It was both terrifying and a relief – an acknowledgement that there was something wrong and more importantly, a chance to get well.

Following my diagnosis – I won't lie to you – I struggled. I was given the name of a condition, I was regarded as safe enough to be back in the community and I was sent home with a promise of a follow-up appointment and the occasional visit from a psychiatric nurse. But no one advised me on what to do. No one told me what to expect, how to manage it or more importantly, what I could do to stay well. So I struggled on in a haze of relief, that what I had experienced was real and had a name, but covering the haze was a fog; a dense fog of not knowing, of not understanding and moreover, of not having the power to do anything to help myself.

Mental health services have come on leaps and bounds since then, and what is now hopefully used is a model of treatment around recovery; taking steps to live as full and responsible a life as possible. However, at the time of my diagnosis, I felt lost and unsure of what to do. I started to treat myself. This is possibly why people describe me as having such good insight and managing so well. It is also what has inspired me to write this.

I have always been bookish and soak up new facts and information with relish. I have always read since I was a young girl. I enjoy the escape and the pleasure of reading. I love absorbing new information, and this has never left me. Thank goodness for that, as it led me to recovery and being my own bipolar life coach. So in the dense fog, I went back to what I had always known, and I started to read. I have never stopped.

I read and read. It almost became an obsession. What was this condition? Why did I have it? How would people react? Was my life over? I went through so many emotions and read the good, the bad and the garbage. If you do research your condition, you will find that there is a litany of material, from dense medical studies, shrouded in words one doesn't understand, to self-help books, biographies and more scarily, people out there who are trying to make a quick buck from your recent diagnosis. Therefore, these should be approached with an open mind, a desire to learn more and a pinch of caution. I do not seek to recommend any particular publication as this would take the power away from you and your freedom of choice. What I do seek to do in this book is to let you know what I have learnt and how you can incorporate this into your life; by becoming your own bipolar life coach.

The getting and staying well will be the theme throughout this book. It translates into self-management, not cure. It is a mix of insight, knowledge, education, empowerment, responsibility, positivity and the strength to ask for help.

The first positive step is to understand your diagnosis. You are likely to be diagnosed as having bipolar disorder. However, there are different types and your particular form of the illness may be deemed to be a specific type[3]. It would be beneficial if you knew which type you most likely have. Do not be afraid to ask your doctor which camp you may fall into, as this is important in learning about your condition and staying well. It is also important to note that not all experiences of mania are about euphoria or extreme risk-taking behaviour. Mania or a 'high' can manifest itself in the form of agitation, inflated ego, anger or vastly increased productivity.

Since my diagnosis, I have never experienced such phenomenal highs as I did in the days before. Self-management and medication has played a huge part in this. I typically experience something called hypomania, which can be evidenced, in my case, as pressured speech, sleeplessness, irritation, increased productivity, inflated ego and increased humour, but is not comparable with the extreme manias of my earlier years. These included almost fantasist behaviours, increased sexual activity and severe risk-taking behaviour. For some, such highs can turn into criminal behaviours in which the individual, when well, would never engage.

Learning about your condition and getting the views of mental health professionals on how it manifests itself is an essential and key element in moving forward into recovery. I have been blessed with some of the most knowledgeable and learned mental health professionals, but this has not always been my experience, and so it is important to conduct research into your condition from reputable sources.

There are a number of fantastic sources of information out there and some wonderful publications, so research these well. There are also free information leaflets available from mental health charities and help lines. Some useful UK-based charities are listed below:

www. bipolaruk. org. uk

www. mind. org. uk

www. rethink. org

Top Tips and Key Action Points:
- Understand your diagnosis.
- Do not ignore your diagnosis – it is the starting point of recovery.
- Don't be afraid to ask questions.

- If necessary, ask for additional appointments and second opinions.
- In the UK, NICE (National Institute for Clinical Excellence) can provide information on what to expect from treatment in the NHS; in other countries, you should contact your health care provider to find out exactly what you are entitled to in terms of care, relapse, treatment and so on.
- Research your condition – use multiple sources, as not all will work for you.
- Educate yourself.

CHAPTER TWO

Medication

I am not going to attempt to advise on medication – that is for the medical experts to do. What I do advise though, is to educate yourself about medication. You will be told about medication and how it can help manage your condition, promote recovery and prevent further episodes or at least reduce their extremity.

An important question to contemplate is how you feel about medication. You may have been admitted to a psychiatric ward and given medication, whether you liked it or not. You may have been so desperate that you would have tried anything to stop these mood swings. I know that at times, I have been so desperate for help that I would have tried anything. I would have taken anything in the hope that it would work and turn my thoughts off. You may be thinking that medication is not for you; you may be feeling scared. It is understandable to be fearful of what medication may do to you.

When I first started presenting to my GP with feelings of low mood, it was suggested I try an anti-depressant.

I was sceptical and scared. I had been brought up in a world where to express sadness was seen as weak and where there was a pressure to pretend all was OK. I was frightened of what taking anti-depressant medication symbolised. Would I become addicted? Was I mad? Did this mean I could not cope with life? Why could I not just pull myself together? Surely if I took this medication, it was like giving in and that would be bad, right? *No!* But in my youth, my ignorance, and my fear, and as a result of my experiences to date, I decided not to go ahead with taking what had been prescribed. This was despite having experienced a tendency to depression and changing moods since my early teenage years.

After about a month, I was seen by a GP who immediately contacted the local psychiatric facility for my admittance. My chat with the GP revealed that I had not eaten or slept in weeks, and had taken to sitting in the dark, unwashed and chain smoking with the doors locked and the curtains closed because they (whoever they were) were coming for me. I was severely depressed and paranoid. I had stood over a partner's sleeping head with a knife, wondering how quiet I could be in killing myself so that by the time he woke up, it would be too late to help me. I was confused, I was scared and I was strange. At this point, the decision to take or not take medication had become irrelevant, and I was taken to the local psychiatric facility and put on medication. However, it was a further two years before I was correctly diagnosed. This level of medication was not compatible with bipolar disorder and it was not really until this diagnosis that I had the chance to get the right medication and to turn my life around.

My point? Sometimes deciding whether to take medication becomes arbitrary and it becomes a matter of life or death. My other point, and I am not pill-pushing here, is that without modern medicine and medication, I am 100% sure I would not be here – I would have taken my own life. So my fear of medication was gone as I began to see its benefits.

As for the fear of others and their opinions as to what my medication means for them, well I can't legislate for that and have finally come around to the thinking that I can give people information – it is up to them whether they decide to accept that I take medication. They have not lived what I have lived and they cannot possibly know the fear of becoming that unwell again or know that my quality of life, my achievements and my pleasure in living life are partly down to modern medicine.

I would never tell a diabetic not to take insulin; would never tell someone with cancer not to give radiation a go. I would never imply that someone who was short-sighted could achieve perfect vision just through positive thinking alone. This is not to say that medication is a cure or indeed the end of the story in managing bipolar disorder. But medication is a personal decision and between you and your mental health team. It is also a journey of trial and error, and so do expect things to stall or to not suit you – just keep at it and you will hopefully find something of benefit to you.

However, the main point of being your own bipolar life coach is about self-management, self-care and recovery, and this is largely to do with mind set, a healthy inner life and positive steps you can take to manage your condition. Am I not, therefore, contradicting myself? Well in a word, no. Medication can be and for many is important in managing their condition and their moods, and in my experience, has often stopped things getting a whole lot worse. But it is not the full picture and lazy mental health treatment and advice is purely based around medication. There is so much more we can do through knowing our condition, coaching ourselves and changing our mind set, and we come to this in the following chapters.

You may prefer not to take medication for whatever reason. You may feel your moods are not so severe that you need medication. You may worry it will alter your personality or what makes you, you. You may feel that you enjoy your moods and that they fuel your creativity or enjoyment of life. Again, this is a personal choice, and no one should interpret this chapter as advocating medication or not. But keep an open mind and if you are deciding to take medication, get clued up.

Medication with any mental health condition is trial and error. There is no one size fits all. Psychiatrists can only judge progress and recovery by what they observe in terms of your presenting mood and behaviour. One major thing they rely on is what you tell them. Therefore, it is imperative that you know what your medication is for and what it is envisaged it will do.

One of the more common treatments for bipolar disorder is a mood stabiliser. Again, your psychiatrist will decide, hopefully through discussions with you, the best form of treatment. Many people are also prescribed an anti-depressant as part of a combination of medications. Be patient with medication. It has taken me a number of years to really start to understand what works for me.

Thinking logically, bipolar disorder is two opposing poles of mood; one low and one high. However, all experiences are different. Some people may have a stronger tendency to low mood and vice-versa. Therefore your prescription should be an individual one that is best suited to your experiences. Again, knowing what your experiences are and learning about your moods is invaluable in finding a drugs combination that works for you.

At different times in my life and my mood, I have taken different medications in varying amounts. When starting to go high, I have been given additional medications to try and prevent this or at least take the edge off and slow it down. This is often a drug I don't take on a regular basis, but one that I take as and when needed. When I have experienced a mania or hypomania, I may have increased my mood stabiliser for a number of months to attempt to prevent going 'up' again. However, the flip side of this is that a high (mania or hypomania) is, for me, always followed by a low or at least the very real threat of a low. Therefore in discussions with my psychiatrist we have to decide what the best course of action is. Do I increase my anti-depressants to stave off a depression, or will this increase in feel-good chemicals tip me back into a high? This constant battle with my mood and trying to anticipate what my bipolar disorder will do next is exhausting, frustrating and essential. In being your own bipolar life coach, you will need to understand your moods, any patterns and your medication.

It is this that you should take away from this section of the book. Know your mood, know your medication and know what to do. Easier said than done? Yes! So how did I go from someone who had never heard of bipolar disorder to someone who is described as having good insight and the ability to manage her condition well? I took the control back, I decided to have a power struggle with my condition, but most of all, I accepted it.

So, what medication and treatment is best for you? I don't know! What I do know is that monitoring your mood; your medication and its effects are key to remaining well. Do your research and have the confidence to ask questions and to try new things with the supervision of your mental health team.

I manage on a therapeutic dose of an anti-depressant and a mood stabiliser. I feel happy with this now, but after more than a decade, it has taken time and toil to get here. I have been on different types of medication and different doses throughout my journey with bipolar disorder, and this will continue to change and evolve.

Next time I feel a high coming on, I may increase my mood stabiliser or take a one-off dose of another drug for a couple of days to try and stop a hypomania. I may experience a deep depression in a few years and need to increase my anti-depressant. My current dose and type of drug may stop working for me altogether and I will need, under the supervision of my psychiatrist, to have a complete medication overhaul. In the next decade, new drugs may become available and I may switch to them.

One of the singularly most important things I have done in terms of medication is that I have observed my psychiatrists and mental health team – when a certain thing happened, what did they do with my medication? What did they want to achieve with any changes, and did they achieve it? I have always asked questions and sought clarification, probably driving them to distraction on some occasions – but I have learnt a great deal this way and made notes.

I am now in the fortunate position where I have a healthy relationship with my psychiatrist and one that, I hope, is based on mutual respect. I often contact him to say what I think needs to be adjusted and will request an appointment when I think action should be taken. This has only come about in recent years, after educating myself and getting to know both bipolar disorder and my medication.

I may one day manage my condition so well that I stop taking medication altogether, but this is not something I see happening anytime soon. I know what works for me. I have read of people who do not take medication and just go with the moods as they come. To me, this seems like a great experiment and can, for many, be the source of brilliance and creativity. It is also one that I will not be testing a hypothesis for anytime soon – not whilst I have a 9-5 job and a mortgage. I cannot take chances on my moods.

Medication is not for everyone, and I know of many success stories where individuals have managed their condition solely via other means. I celebrate this and admire them and I am getting there. I am on the lowest dose of my life and am living my life positively. This is through the self-management and lifestyle techniques that I go on to explore in the coming chapters.

But it was medication that meant I could recover enough to learn more about my condition, be able to work again, enjoy independence and intellectual outlets. It allowed me to take time to gain the knowledge and insight needed to be able to manage on a significantly lowered dose.

Another important reason for knowing your medication takes me back to one of my original points. Your medical team will rely on you to help them achieve the correct level of medication. Therefore, you are a key component in their assessments. You should know your moods and log your feelings so that you can feed back to them. You may only be seen for a short appointment every few months, and so keeping an open dialogue about your daily experiences is essential.

Top Tips and Key Action Points:

- Know what your medication is, including expected side effects, and know what it is meant to be doing.
- Know when you should be taking it.
- Know when it is likely to start benefitting you – some medications can take a while to get into your system.
- Know what each different medication does and how it

interacts – know when you need to change, increase or decrease it.

- Observe your psychiatrist and mental health team – they have trained and continue to train for the knowledge that you need. Ask questions, learn, revisit and ask again.
- Equip yourself with the knowledge of what you should and should not do when taking a particular drug, such as driving, drinking and even getting pregnant.
- Keep a diary, a checklist, a file on your smart phone … whatever works for you in order to monitor medication and its effects, both positive and negative. This is a good way of starting to get to know your medication and can put you on the road to managing it yourself and being able to identify when a change needs to happen.

Whilst confidence and self-management are key to recovery, remember that bipolar disorder is a serious and enduring mental illness and that sometimes you will not recognise you are high or low. Always seek the appropriate medical support and advice and keep in regular contact with your mental health team.

CHAPTER THREE

Looking Beyond Medication into Acceptance and Towards Recovery

Medication is just part of the picture. Whilst I am grateful for the freedom modern medicine has given me, it is only a part of what I do to manage my condition and be my own bipolar life coach.

I do not attempt to take away any credit from pharmaceutical companies and what they have given me – or the psychiatrists and nurses who have helped me enormously over the years, but they are only part of the answer. You may not automatically be told this, but I am telling you now!

I have described how I read and researched and read again. I was hungry for information on what I could do as an individual to manage my condition. If I am honest, I also felt so angry at the card I had been dealt that it spurred me on. I wanted control and I wanted the power back. I wanted my life back and I wanted to be normal. This was naïve thinking and eventually I started to accept that I could not change this and I could not make it go away.

I have always felt a little different to others and have come to accept that I am not normal, whatever that means. I often feel like a square peg in a world of round holes and to try to be exactly like everyone else is fruitless. So I wasted a little time railing against my diagnosis, ignoring really thinking about it in the hope that it would go away. I tried to live like I had always done and lo and behold, I came unstuck time and time again.

However, this was an important part of my recovery, in that I had to come to my own conclusions about this. I could read all I wanted and could learn as much theory as was out there, but what was missing was me. I needed to accept this and realise this was who I was before anything could really work or treat me. I had to accept it, or how could I expect others to?

Eventually I got there, and you will also need to. I looked bipolar disorder in the eye, and to my horror, realised it had a steadier gaze than I. It was this realisation that almost made me think, "game over". I could have easily tipped over into being the victim and given myself over to this condition, but deep down I knew I wanted more from life. So what? Did I fight it? No, I looked back at it and held its gaze. I didn't fight it, but I also didn't let it win. I held my hand out to it and made friends. I decided to respect it and to start to discover how we could cohabit as harmoniously as possible. Like any relationship or marriage, it needs work, nurture and respect. Now, when I feel an episode coming on, I open the door to it and say, "Hello old friend, you are welcome here". But what I don't do is give in to it. I also don't fight it, but I do work with it and use the tried and tested techniques that, for me, have worked wonders over years.

It may seem strange to some, but my bipolar disorder is like an imaginary friend from childhood: we talk, we experience things together and we are comfortable in each other's company. No one can see our relationship, because it is unique to us and invisible to others. I accept now I have bipolar disorder and it is possibly one of the few constants in my life. It will not leave me and it will not go away. So I have given it the respect it deserves because it is so powerful it can sometimes take my breath away.

If there is one thing you can take away from reading this, it is that bipolar disorder is a condition for which there is currently no cure. You are always at risk of an episode. Therefore, one of the best ways to stay well is to welcome it, embrace it, make peace with it and then learn how to live with it. Like any relationship, there are times when you will differ, when you quarrel and when you forget to make time for each other, and in the end the relationship suffers and things can turn ugly. So respect, acceptance, acknowledgement and care are the best approach.

This nicely leads me into the main purpose of this book, which is to be your own bipolar life coach. Over the coming chapters, we will look at different methods and approaches I have used, and you, too, can adopt, to start *living* with bipolar disorder and managing it. We will look at alternative therapies and their place, monitoring your mood, knowing your triggers, managing your relationships with others, communication and lifestyle choices. You cannot tackle any of these things if you do not make peace with bipolar disorder and accept it.

Top Tips and Key Action Points:

- Make peace with bipolar disorder.
- Learn more about it.
- *Accept it and start to move forward positively.*

You have been given this unique condition and should start to work on your relationship with it. You are going to be in this relationship for the rest of your life – there is no divorce, no time out, and no trial separation and so the only approach is nurture and respect.

CHAPTER FOUR

Talking Therapies

There are currently many studies and websites discussing how many words a day the average person speaks. When I have been manic or hypomanic, there have not been enough minutes in the day to get out what I wanted to say, and when I'm depressed, there is so much destructive dialogue inside my head that to utter anything would take too much energy.

But the important thing is that we do talk; we do communicate. This is and has always been an essential part of the human condition. Make your words count. This is not some bumper sticker for world peace, but sensible advice to anyone considering talking therapy or any form of psychological therapy. You may want to ask your mental health team about what talking or psychological therapies are available to you. Talking therapies are not for everyone, but they helped me enormously.

I have struggled with writing this book for a while now, and that is because, for it to really benefit people, I think it should be honest. My intention is not to hurt anyone, but I do feel that sharing common experiences is an important part of recovery and the real purpose of this book. We are all human and to be human is to feel. To feel is to feel not only joy, but also fear, anger, loathing, despair and hurt. If we didn't feel such emotions, then many of the great poets, playwrights and authors that have been celebrated throughout history would have had little to write about. It is what we do with these feelings that is important. Our experiences shape most of us, and sometimes we need to acknowledge which of these is causing us distress.

The information I have gathered over the years as to the causes of bipolar disorder is inconclusive, but I would recommend that you look into the results of research and, like me, become involved in it. There is currently excellent research being done into genetics, environmental factors, hormones, brain chemicals and the causes of bipolar disorder.

There are so many variables that nothing can yet be discounted or ignored, but there is no getting away from the fact that we are the sum of our experiences. Whether these are the cause of bipolar disorder or feature more prominently in our thoughts and behaviours because we have bipolar disorder is yet to be determined. One thing that was highlighted by one particularly excellent psychiatrist who treated me was that a common theme in some bipolar disorder patients is certain early experiences. We have all had experiences that have affected our mental health, whether we have a diagnosis of mental illness or not. A common theme during a depressive phase can be to remember significant events and unanswered and unacknowledged hurts.

These can be significant to people with bipolar disorder or depression, and dealing with them can be beneficial. Such was the significance during my episodes that – like the very existence of bipolar disorder itself – I could no longer ignore what they were doing to me, so I sought help. Being your own bipolar life coach is about taking control and looking forward, but sometimes we need to look back in order to move positively into the future.

I asked for a referral for counselling and the results were truly life changing – it was a confidential and safe environment where nothing and no one was off limits. At first, it was an opportunity to let off steam and make sense of my life in general. However, as luck would have it, during my treatment I experienced a full-blown episode. During the depression that followed, my counselling took on a whole new life, and the thoughts, voices, experiences and emotions that plagued me were talked about and acknowledged.

It was a gift to have such intense counselling during a depressive phase. I took my experiences out of the box in which I had tried to shut them away and I held them in my hand and my heart and I looked at them. I relived them, which was painful, but also cathartic. I wrote letters to significant people in my life (which were never mailed) and to myself, at different periods during my life, and started to deal with it all. It was a long road and it definitely got worse before it got better, but it really did change my life and my outlook.

Why? I acknowledged what was causing pain and confusion and accepted it. Although those experiences and feelings did not completely go away, I discovered techniques to help deal with them if they returned, and I began to let them go. They were weighing me down – they were part of my past, but did they really have to be part of my future? I could not carry these feelings around with me any longer, and nor could I look to others to make me happy.

Another benefit of counselling was that I began to see my behaviours in the past for what they were. For some reason, I had been under the impression that I was not loveable and had been trying to fill that void. I had been striving to keep the upper hand in romantic relationships. Criticising was my way of preventing being hurt. I pushed people away because fundamentally I felt unlovable and unworthy of true, respectful and balanced love. This is a common theme for many people who experience depression and talking about it puts it out in the open, where it can be examined.

I also started to try to forgive myself. I had caused hurt with my destructive behaviours and I needed to send out a silent prayer to those I had hurt, acknowledging my behaviour and asking for their forgiveness. If you are one of these people, I am sorry. I also caused a wake of destruction in some of my serious manic phases, from funny anecdotes of swearing or over-sharing in a formal environment to inappropriate and risk-taking behaviour that caused hurt to others. I had uttered words that were cruel and unkind and I could not take them back, but I did have to start accepting this and start to forgive myself.

Counselling was an opportunity to reconnect with my true self; the person I wanted and deserved to be. It was a chance to live my life in line with what I believed to be true: that love, encouragement and a healthy emotional life were the keys to a life well lived and a condition well managed.

It should be noted that this chapter is not written to garner sympathy and pity – it is to help you identify and look at what is troubling you. I have had a good life and have not experienced the unimaginable horrors and traumas that many people with and without bipolar disorder have experienced. This chapter is aimed at acknowledging what damages us and what holds us back, no matter how trivial or self-absorbed it may seem to the outside and untrained eye. If you feel it; it is real to you, if it is holding you back, then address it.

Once my counselling had finished, I was inspired to look at what else could help me. I researched cognitive behavioural therapy (CBT), and my reading around this translated into me adopting some of the basic principles of this technique and led me on to life coaching. All these theories and techniques are, in short, about changing your reaction to things, challenging your thought processes and replacing them with something more positive. In life, there will always be external forces that will influence you. Talking therapies can help change your reaction to these.

I began to understand how a great deal of the anxiety I experienced as part of my condition was learned behaviour – the feeling that something bad could always happen if we didn't control every minutiae of life was overwhelming. In the end, I decided to reject this message of panic and fear. After a long journey with self-taught coaching and CBT, I came to accept that one of the great joys of life was to rejoice in surprise. I accepted that the world did not revolve around me and that I really, really, really had to stop worrying about the small stuff.

Now I always try to look at a situation with a practical outlook. I ask myself what I can do to resolve an issue. In many cases, there is nothing I can do, so I go with it. If I am stuck in a traffic jam, there is nothing I can do about it, so rather than go into a spin, I tune the radio in to a favourite station and enjoy the music. I have discovered that some people stress over the small things in life to avoid having to deal with the big.

What should you take away from this chapter about being your own bipolar life coach? Episodes may keep happening and the same feelings, experiences and emotions may keep coming to the surface to be relived and to cause further hurt. Talking therapy is not for everyone, but for some, it does help, and I found it to be life-changing. But be warned, talking therapies are a very personal decision and a personal journey. It can be a painful and introspective process and get worse before it gets better. If you are interested, however, your mental health team will be able to tell you what is available in your area.

Top Tips and Key Action Points:

- Talk to your mental health team about the options available to you and read up on the therapies you are considering. There are a variety of different types and approaches. Some of the main ones are counselling, psychotherapy, and cognitive behavioural therapy. There are also less commonly known therapies, such as mindfulness-based therapy and many more[4.]
- If you are sourcing a talk therapist privately, make sure practitioners are suitably qualified.
- You must be ready to talk – you cannot move forward if you are not prepared to be honest with yourself.
- Start to acknowledge what emotions and experiences may be troubling you. Accepting these will help you move forward.
- As you are going through your therapy, make notes on what you have discovered – they may come in handy in the future when you are experiencing an episode or slipping into old behaviours.
- Learn and listen. Be open to new ways of thinking and changing thought patterns and behaviours.
- Forget stigma – remember that it takes courage and strength to acknowledge our inner life.

CHAPTER FIVE

Know Your Triggers

Medication and talking therapies may be the sum of what you will be told about living with bipolar disorder. They are, as discussed, important options in the treatment of bipolar disorder. However, through my journey, I wanted to learn more and started to educate myself about how I could be my own bipolar life coach.

It is important to note that self-management and being your own bipolar life coach is a personal process – we all experience our condition differently. What many medical professionals and I agree on is that insight and understanding are important. Unfortunately, the severity of our moods can mean that on occasion, we cannot see what is happening and so cannot put things in place. This is where educating those around us is an essential part of managing, and maintaining close links with your mental health team remains one of the best things you can do.

It should be noted that these tips will be most useful for those who have bipolar disorder Type 1 or Type 2. Those who experience rapid cycling may find other literature more helpful.

The information may also be useful for people who suffer from unipolar depression, as many of the techniques and considerations remain the same.

It is increasingly accepted that many episodes whether they be manic, hypomanic or depressive are preceded by triggers. My triggers may be different to yours, and so this is where monitoring and education are important. Highlighting your triggers can help you plan, anticipate possible outcomes and put things in place such as seeking support, telling your mental health team or reassessing the many demands in your life.

Life is full of surprises – therein lies its beauty. If we knew exactly what was going to happen and could accurately predict the future, much of the joy of life would disappear. We cannot avoid certain events and change is the only constant, so trying to avoid everything, everyone and every eventuality would be exhausting and, frankly, impossible. What we can do is plan as much as possible, learn from how we have overcome things in the past and learn from our mistakes.

Look back and start to analyse when episodes or feelings similar to those experienced in an episode have begun. What was going on in your life at that time? Can you see any patterns? Do those around you see any patterns when your mood takes a turn for the worse?

Remember that bipolar disorder is complex, and it may not be specific events that are to blame for an episode or change in mood, but the reaction to the event. For example, a boss who criticises your work a lot may bring to the surface feelings of inadequacy or criticism from childhood.

To do this, you do not need to look at your entire life in minute detail, but try and draw up some sort of timeline, even if it is just for your most recent episode in the first instance. It can be useful to draw up a table or something pictorial – whatever works for you. Below is an example of a simple table that might help prompt you to fill in the gaps. The more you do this, the more likely you are to see a pattern or common triggers.

Did you have a big project due at college or in the work place? Had your workload or responsibilities increased?

Was there conflict within your relationship or your wider family?

Was your general health suffering? Had a physical or chronic complaint impacted on you? Were concerns for someone else's health taking their toll on you?

Had there been a major shift is relationship dynamics – for example, the break-up of a long-term relationship or the decision to get married, cohabit or start a family? Had your partner been made redundant, placing more financial pressure on you?

Were external forces playing a part – for example, financial worries, or were you trying to sell a house? Had you been affected by crime?

FACTORS IN THE LEAD-UP TO MY EPISODE(S)						
GENERAL HEALTH	MAJOR LIFE EVENTS	RELATIONSHIP	FAMILY	WORK/ STUDY	EXTERNAL EVENTS	CHANGES IN MEDICATION OR THERAPIES

Top Tips and Key Action Points:

- Start to identify your triggers.
- Build up a picture. It may feel like a jigsaw puzzle with no picture to copy at first, but it will hopefully start to make sense.
- If they are open to it, get input from others in your life.
- Be open to exploring your inner self again. It may not be the event that is the root cause, but the feelings it stirs up in you.

CHAPTER SIX

Mood Diary

Another way to get to know your triggers, moods and danger points can be by keeping a diary or journal. It could be in-depth or just noting what is happening in your life and how this is making you feel. Start small and don't pressure yourself to get it right first time. I certainly didn't. A cruel trick of bipolar disorder is that if we are experiencing a high, we may not see that anything is wrong. My highs can creep up gradually. The desire to feel good, efficient, and confident has fuelled the self-help industry in the developed world; why would we be concerned about feeling good? The thing is, if you have bipolar disorder, it may not stop at feeling good – and the effects can be devastating.

I mentioned earlier that I feel like a square peg in a world of round holes, and this is a cruel by-product of bipolar disorder – normal human emotions can mean more for me. One of my regrets in managing my condition well is that I feel I have sanitised who I am. I look at my moods and emotions and try to categorise them. This saddens me, but it is a necessary part of remaining well and living a full life. Reducing the amount and severity of episodes I experience means I get more from life and stay alive.

A mood diary can be a positive step to recovery. Different methods work for different people, so try them out and see how you feel. I have seen a number of ways to record mood during the course of my life with bipolar disorder. Many that are published can look daunting, and so I have included some more simple methods. These exercises can help identify any warning signs before you reach crisis point, allowing you to put appropriate measures in place.

Scale of one to ten

Three times a day, I mark myself against a simple scale of one to ten. This allows me to see any patterns or concerns:

1	2	3	4	5	6	7	8	9	10
Suicidal		Low		Balanced		High		Mania	

The trick here is to remember that all human beings have days or moments when they feel happy and low. Part of the human condition is to feel, and so if you have a day when you feel joy – for example, watching your daughter graduate, finding out you got the job, having that great first date or seeing your favourite comedian does not mean you are automatically going manic. Similarly, we all have days when we can feel low. We may have received upsetting news, failed a test or had a row with our partner. The trick is to see patterns and a lack of balance in mood that is starting to affect your behaviour.

Dear Diary

Some people keep an actual diary to help monitor mood. This may not be for you, and you may find it too time-consuming, but for those for whom it works, it really works. Not only is it a great way to keep track of your mood, but writing down experiences and thoughts can be extremely therapeutic and help us to make sense of our lives. The top tip here is to set boundaries.

If you are going to write down all your thoughts are there certain people in your lives who you would prefer not to read these? If so, keep it locked, password protected, or hidden. Alternatively, you may want a partner, close friend, carer, talk therapist, nurse or psychiatrist to read your diary as a way of monitoring your mood, and this should be agreed with them. Do what feels right for you.

More Complex Mood Charts

Do your own research – there may be other more complex mood charts that work for you, and you may feel that the more information you can collect, collate and analyse, the better you can manage your condition.

You could devise a chart that combines life events and external factors, your mood and reactions to them and what medication or other treatments you are using. This can be a useful way of looking at what, if anything, different treatments are doing and how they are helping, and empower you to start to learn when they need tweaking. None of these factors are mutually exclusive in managing bipolar disorder, and so it can be useful to get an overall picture.

You may wish to do this using a simple chart with columns for each, as below:

	Anti-Dep Dose	Mood Stab Dose	Talking Therapy	Well-being Activity	Significant Things to Note	Sleep	Mood Score
Mon 1st	20mg	250mg	x	x	x	Fair	5
Tues 2nd	20mg	250mg	Counselling session	Jogging	Difficult feelings around rejection brought up in counselling	Disturbed	4
Weds 3rd	20mg	250mg	x	x	Feeling of sadness from yesterday	Fair	4
Thurs 4th	20mg	250mg	x	x	Had to stay late at work for a meeting	Fair	4
Fri 5th	20mg	250mg	x	Meditation before bed	Relief at end of working week	Fair	5
Sat 6th	20mg	250mg	x	Massage	Disagreement with mum over the phone	Fair	4/5
Sun 7th	20mg	250mg	x	Jogging	Worrying about presentation at work tomorrow	Disturbed	4/5

Some people use computer programmes to record mood, which can then be shown in a variety of formats such as bar charts and graphs (this of course depends on how computer literate you are).

Top Tips and Key Action Points:

- Insight is not automatic – it's something you have to teach yourself.
- Being able to monitor your mood is an excellent tool for self-management.
- Find a system that works for you: use one of these, research a different one or devise your own.
- If it helps, share your mood diary and charts with significant others or professionals.
- Keep at it – you may miss things when starting out. Learn from the process.
- Take action! This is a pointless exercise if you don't use it to your advantage. When patterns or warning signs are there, do something!

CHAPTER SEVEN

Stress

In the previous two chapters, we started to look at events, circumstances and daily living as a way to unlocking the secret to your episodes and moods. This is not a cure-all, but a useful way to start looking at, anticipating and managing your moods.

What is the common theme in the discussion of moods, triggers, and influencing factors? Stress.

Stress and its effects on bipolar disorder are now well documented. My own journey with bipolar disorder has been proof enough of this. Stress always precedes my episodes.

Stress in modern life is widely discussed. But what do we mean by stress? I have a hunch that stress is now an overused word, and often wrongly used for what is a minor annoyance. My work with people has shown that this is a term that is no longer correctly used. People say they were stressed because they had to wait in a long queue at the supermarket or stressed because their internet connection was down for a couple of days.

Due to its overuse, the term "stress" has almost been made meaningless. Certainly, those who are off work with stress or say they can't do something because of stress are often deemed as weak or just not resilient enough to cope with life. I have overheard comments about myself: "What has she got to be stressed about, she should try having two kids?", or, "Well, we are all stressed, we just have to get on with it". Such people do not understand the affects that acute stress can have on those who have a severe and enduring mental illness such as bipolar disorder.

Stress will mean different things to each of us. We all deal with stress differently and all have different thresholds. The trick here is to recognise what is stress to you and what types of things have caused you stress before an episode. A number of years ago, in the space of a couple of months, I went through a separation, bereavement and a house move. I did not have an episode, but when I become acutely stressed in the work place, an episode is sure to follow. When I have had issues with my family, it has brought on an episode. What does this mean for you? Know what is likely to trigger feelings of acute stress and what is not.

I have always put a lot of pressure on myself in terms of work and have a very strong work ethic. I am now more wary about taking on too much or multiple projects at once. The need to please in order to get approval is a theme in many people's lives and an issue that I have had to work on. I have come to realise that taking on a lot of additional work may allow me to temporarily shine, but can also have disastrous consequences.

Like so many of us, my family and I can fall into old patterns. Disagreements tend to bring up old feelings, and I have had to start to recognise these. I am not blaming my family here, but giving the example that we can all fall into old behaviours in significant relationships, and so what I have started to do is change my reaction. Why am I telling you this? To urge you to identify what stress means to you, so you can anticipate when there could be consequences.

What is also important is realising that stress can happen no matter what we do. Being your own bipolar life coach does not mean avoiding all stress and withdrawing from life. Life will always throw things at you. The key is in developing ways to deal with it that are bipolar disorder-friendly.

I am a firm believer in acknowledging your achievements and not being critical. By all means, be reflective, make positive changes and acknowledge your limits, but do not torture yourself about stress. It has been pointed out to me that I deal with a large amount of stress, but this does not stop me being diligent in looking out for stress. I need to catch it before it takes hold. If the warning signs are there, I put in place what is necessary, recognising that I have a unique condition. I would urge you to do the same. In the Lifestyle chapter, we look at ways you can manage your life in order to manage stress.

Top Tips and Key Action Points:

- Moving on from your work on triggers and monitoring your mood, start to identify those things which cause you stress.

- Define your own meanings – what stresses you may not stress me and vice-versa.
- Start to anticipate when stress may be approaching and put things in place to manage it or to get help with it.
- Do not be defined by others' expectations. By being your own bipolar life coach, you are on the road to learning and development and you set the agenda.

CHAPTER EIGHT

A Healthy Inner Life;
Changing Your Thought Processes

Hopefully at this stage, you are now open to discovering more about your condition, what triggers an episode, what stress means for you and what influences your condition. This is knowledge and acceptance. Accepting that you have bipolar disorder and gaining the knowledge and insight as to what triggers an episode is a powerful gift.

Once I had accepted my condition, I began to learn more, and in turn began to understand it. I then started to take action to manage it. In later chapters, we will look at what practical things you can put in place in terms of your daily life. In this section, we are going to look at some ways to start bringing your inner life to a healthier place and using this to manage your bipolar disorder.

For anyone that is familiar with the twelve-step programme for addiction, there is a strong school of thought for accepting the things we cannot change. I am a firm believer in this where appropriate. The things that were tormenting me from my past were relentless during a depression. I have accepted that they are in the past and I cannot change them, but what I haven't done is ignore them. In talking therapies, I got them out and looked at them, made sense of them, and accepted them. It was only when I had done this that I was able to change my reaction to them. These things still cause hurt, but they no longer torture me as my focus is on a positive now and a positive future.

What I can now do is recognise when these early experiences are influencing my present. As a child, I could not make sense of some experiences and as a result, stored them as rejection, which fuelled feelings of insecurity. When we were first living together, I drove my husband to distraction when he was having a quiet moment. He may have had a busy day at work and would just want to eat quietly and watch a football match.

When he was quiet, I used to tie myself in knots asking what was wrong and whether it was something I had done. I now realise he was merely tired and doing what he needed to do for his mental wellbeing, but it took me a while to get there. I was bringing my issues in from the past and letting them be part of my future. Recognising this was empowering for me and I started to realise that, although I could not control my brain or thoughts as such, I could control what to do with them. I could start to change my thought patterns. Much of this technique is rooted in cognitive behavioural therapy (CBT) and again you may want to learn more about this technique.

Your mental health team may be able to refer you for CBT-based treatment, or you could consider life coaching.

I continued my journey into being my own bipolar life coach. Life coaching and CBT are not historic, but forward-looking. Whilst it is important to acknowledge past hurts and experiences, it is not always healthy to remain fixated on them. Counselling and psychotherapy can be useful for identifying and exploring past hurts, but the focus of the coach is about now, the future and improvement.

Our feelings and learned behaviours influence the way we experience things. Many people fear public speaking, but what is the worst that can happen? Why do they feel this? Do they already anticipate rejection, failure and not being able to hold their audience? The professional comedian is desperate to get up in public and be laughed at! In my work with people who have low self-esteem, it is clear that many people are so wrapped up in what might happen were they to do something and it went wrong that it cripples them for most of their lives.

I have coached individuals who have been terrified of public speaking or interviews and have asked them, "What is the worst that can happen? You are laughed out of the room? You don't get the job? So what? Find out why you didn't get then job or were laughed at and work on it."

One technique I have used with young people who are terrified to even say their name in front of a group of people is to get them to build up to doing something stupid in front of a group. It could be to sing a silly song, mime a funny action or do a silly dance. By doing this, they discover that nothing bad happened; they were able to do something and it did not have the consequences they had anticipated. They start to learn not to 'catastrophise'. Changing our mind set is the secret to a healthy inner life.

So what does this mean for you? Once you have recognised your triggers, your stresses and your emotional baggage, change your attitude to them. Know when these things are coming and start to recognise your feeling towards them. I have the mental image of a red flag in my head, and when I start to experience old feelings and attitudes I pause, hold up the red flag and change course. Going back to my example of when my husband is being quiet and my old feelings of rejection and insecurity raise their ugly heads, which they do, I recognise them, pause, hold up my red flag and mentally change course and recognise what is really happening.

An example that will be relevant to most people with bipolar disorder is dealing with feelings of depression. I, for one, have experienced such deep and torturous depressions that I have almost made it my life's work never to go back there. Knowing my warning signs for an episode and having the benefit of insight has been the key in self-coaching and managing my mood.

My episodes tend to follow a pattern: high, then low. Thanks to knowing my condition well, I have in recent years only experienced hypomania, and for this, I am grateful. What normally follows is what I call the feeling of being approached by darkness. I am lucky now that I can identify when this is happening and start to put things in place to minimise it.

In the past, when the darkness was approaching, I felt powerless and sank into it. I didn't really know what was happening and had not acquired any techniques to deal with it. So I did what I had always done and went with it. The result was a deep and dark depression that lasted for a significant period of time and was hard to get out of. What's changed now is my reaction to it. I see the darkness coming and say, "Hello, old friend", but I do everything in my power to change its course. This is not to say I no longer feel low, anxious or depressed, but I have learned techniques to shift the power balance in my favour.

A common experience for me is to feel anxious about social settings once I have had a hypomania and am tipping into depression. This is not always without foundation, as I may feel that I have embarrassed myself socially when hypomanic. I think the natural reaction to this is to want to shrink away and disengage from the world. I am embarrassed, I am scared and I just don't think I can keep doing this – it is too exhausting. So I allow myself a few days' 'time out'. I stay indoors and chill, but what I don't do is sink. I force myself out of bed and believe me, some days, this is no easy task. I almost force feed myself three square meals. I do things – be it watching movies or reading magazines. Sometimes my brain is so tired from hypomania that all I can manage is colouring in with felt pens. I take long baths and I relax.

It is hard to explain to someone who has never experienced a mania the exhaustion that can follow. Your brain and body have been working overtime. I feel like I have done several mental marathons without pause and so need the rest and recuperation. But what I am determined in is that this is rest and recuperation and not permission to sink into depression. So after my time out, I physically get out. I make myself engage with the world, as the more I do this the more familiar it is. Often I only want to go out with my husband with me, but I do something each day, even if it is just a small stroll. Then I build up and challenge myself.

If I am feeling anxious about getting out and mixing with people, I force myself to do it. I start small and build it up. To interact with people, I may start by buying something from a local store. Then I move on to going to bigger stores that I don't know so well. I may still feel anxious, but all the time I am talking to myself. I coach myself through it. I reassure myself of what is the worst that could happen. I keep pausing, holding up my red flag and changing the course of my thoughts.

I can now recognise that depression is looming. I can acknowledge it, identify possible likely scenarios, pause, hold up my red flag and change course. I don't pressure myself too much, feel disappointed in myself, deny my feelings or disrespect my condition.

You, too, can start to implement this into your life. Work on changing your reaction and taking back the control. Practice. Build it up. Accept that there will be tough days ahead and that past hurts will rear their heads. Accept that you will be tempted to go down the negative roads of the past. Once you can accept this will happen and that the brain is a powerful machine, you can accept it is coming, but you do not have to accept what depression is saying. Recognise these thoughts and fears and say hello to them, but do not make them feel at home. Recognise the negative, accept it and then go in the other direction.

Many people with bipolar disorder can experience paranoia or full-blown psychosis. In my early experiences, this just arrived with what seemed like little warning. Now I realise I am given warning. Once I start to experience acute stress and possible hypomania, I am lying in wait for any paranoia. It is crafty and it starts small. It can reveal itself in the look from a shop assistant or a comment from a colleague. In the past, I would have completely believed my feelings and accepted them as real, justifying my reaction. But now I have accepted that paranoia might come, I can watch out for it.

Now, when I have these feelings I pause, hold up the red flag, and change course. Don't get me wrong – there will be days when a shop assistant is sneering at me and a colleague makes a genuinely nasty comment aimed at hurting me. The trick here is to discern whether it is happening or is just in my head, so I change my feelings towards it and thus my response. Can I control that a shop assistant thinks I am not skinny or rich enough for her goods? Er, no. Can I control what a colleague says? Again, no. Where does my power lie? In changing my reaction to it.

Accepting the things we cannot change is a true gift in working towards a healthier inner life. Learning to change our reaction and almost completely reject certain pre-programmed feelings is priceless. This is a technique that can be hard to master, so start small. Below are a few examples of scenarios where an individual has the power to change their reaction to what is causing pain.

Rose always feels stressed about spending Christmas with her family. She feels that her mother criticises her life, and her mother is particularly upset that Rose is still single at the age of 37.

1) *Before the holidays, Rose recognises that this may be a trigger for her and will definitely be a source of stress.*
2) *Rose starts to think about the possible scenarios that could occur and some possible responses. Rose knows if she answers back too much, this will cause an argument, so she starts to think of mantras she can say to herself.*
3) *Before the holidays, Rose spends time with friends who accept her, so she feels good about herself.*
4) *When her mother arrives, Rose has everything prepared and feels calm.*
5) *Rose's mother starts to tell her about a second cousin who has recently become engaged. Rose mentally rolls her eyes, but instead of rising to the bait, says she is thrilled for the cousin.*
6) *Rose's mother again talks about her single status. Rose pauses, holds up her red flag and says that she may one day like to meet someone, but only someone that makes her truly happy; she will not settle for less. She*

tells her mother about how much she is getting out of her life right now. Rose then changes the subject.

On previous Christmases, Rose would have had a huge row with her mother, been in tears, felt inadequate, and gotten extremely stressed, and this would have had a significant impact on her mental health. This Christmas, Rose identified her triggers and likely outcomes and prepared accordingly. As a result, her mother behaved the same as always, but the outcome for Rose's mental health was entirely different. Rose accepted that she could not change her mother's behaviour and so changed her reaction to it. She successfully became her own bipolar life coach.

Geoff had experienced a large amount of work related stress due to his employer merging with another company. This period was unsettling for Geoff and he had been worried about possible redundancies. His sleep was affected and he was concerned he may be leading up to an episode. He experienced some feelings of slight mania and so decided to take a few weeks' leave from work. Once he was off work, feelings of low mood started to come in and was waking early yet not wanting to get out of bed. Geoff started to think familiar thoughts about how useless he was for feeling low and how his father had been right – that he wasn't a real man because he felt depressed.

The difference this time was that Geoff recognised that these feelings always started to creep in when he was feeling low. Geoff accepted that the feelings were part of his pattern in depression. Previously, Geoff would have tortured himself with these feelings of inadequacy, but now he recognised what they were. They were the opinions of someone who did not understand or was scared of mental illness. They did not mean that Geoff was not a real man or that he was weak, and he used some of the tips he gained in counselling to work through them.

Geoff found it easier to make sense of his feelings when he wrote them down. He compared his notes to the last time he felt low and found that there were very similar themes and topics. Geoff had the insight to note that these were just his condition talking and that when well, he did not give such thoughts or opinions any credit.

During the next few weeks, when Geoff experienced these feelings and thoughts, he paused, held up his red flag, and changed course, acknowledging these feelings for what they were. This was a real challenge, and Geoff still felt low, but this time, his episode was not so deep. He no longer tortured himself with messages from the past which previously contributed to his depressive phases and led into a spiral of negative thinking and self-loathing. Geoff had successfully coached himself!

———————————————

Marion found it hard to take a compliment and lacked confidence. Marion almost enjoyed her mania because she felt more confident during such phases. When stable, Marion decided to work on her feelings of *low confidence. She started to recognise where these messages came from.*

Marion decided to take up a new hobby to boost her confidence, and joined the jogging club at her local support group. This allowed her to meet other people with similar experiences, so she felt accepted. Seeing how she progressed with her running gave her more confidence. Marion decided to ask her friends to all think of one thing they valued her for. She then noted these things down and read them every time she started to feel low in confidence. These became like a mantra for her and after reading them so many times, she memorised them.

Every time Marion started to be concerned about her abilities and her value, she paused, held up her red flag, recognised these thoughts and changed their meaning by repeating some of the lovely things her friends said: "Sally thinks I am a good listener", "Richie was really grateful for the support I gave him when his mum was ill", "Penny thinks the way I tell my anecdotes from work are funny", "Cheryl thinks I am a great cook". Marion coached herself to a more positive outlook!

Top Tips and Key Action Points:

- Use your mood diary and your knowledge of triggers and stress to help with your progress to a healthier inner life. Start to look at common patterns in the way something made you feel. Did you have to feel this way, or did you have any power?
- Develop your own red flag system – anything that works for you and symbolises taking a moment to stop and look at what is happening.

- Work on your inner life: explore where negative feelings are coming from and consider how you can change them.
- Like Marion, start to gather information on your qualities and gifts. These can be a comfort and also the basis of an inner mantra of positivity.
- Negative messages from the past do not have to be part of your future. Take the power back by consciously rejecting them when they arise.
- Start to be forward-looking: you cannot change your past; you can only steer your future.
- Bipolar disorder is a huge part of your life, granted. The trick is to know it, to accept it and to work with it.
- Be one step ahead of your depression: take time out, recognise it, feel comforted in its predictability, but do not sink. Be forward-looking, but don't fight back by trying to ignore it.
- Recognise depression and paranoia, respect them and learn new techniques to address them.
- Take time out to deal with an episode – ignoring it and soldiering on will not prevent it.
- Accept these things take time. There is no magic answer; I am still learning, but each time an episode comes, I am more prepared, never go higher or lower than the last time and recover more quickly, therefore it is worth it.

CHAPTER NINE

Responsibility

Responsibility is a scary word for many, but it also implies power and positivity. I have bipolar disorder. It can be brutal and I cannot get rid of it, but what I can do is take responsibility for myself and my life with it.

When manic or depressed, I can genuinely say I have done, said and thought things that I had no control over. My behaviours and thoughts were out of control, as was my compass for what was normal behaviour for me. I remember one psychiatric nurse saying she did not believe I had no control and she didn't really buy into my manic phase.

My response at the time was to further punish myself with the feelings of guilt and self-loathing that came after mania and during a depression. All I can say now is I don't really believe in her ability as a mental health professional. But the important point at that time was that I did not know I had bipolar disorder and therefore it was not treated, medicated and more importantly, was nowhere close to being controlled.

However, once I was diagnosed, like anyone with the condition, I knew that I was not crazy. This comes with feelings of relief and terror. I knew I had a condition, but I didn't really accept it and I certainly did not respect it. The result was more episodes and madness. Only when I accepted it could I deal with it and start to shift the power balance. By researching my condition and learning about it, I started to get insight and understanding. I could make changes to my life and outlook that could not cure this thing, but could make it more manageable and in turn, improve my quality of life. Without insight, there is little we can do. With insight, the possibilities are endless.

Hopefully at this stage, you are starting to think about changes you can make and things you can introduce to learn about your condition and start to get some control back. Reread the chapters on therapies, treatments, monitoring your mood and gaining a healthy inner life if you need to. These are what lead us from acceptance and through to responsibility.

I have not bought into the idea that this thing controls me completely. It is a huge part of who I am and it will never go away, granted. I should ignore it at my peril as it will control me and it will ruin me. But what I have done is moved from accepting it into managing it; this is taking responsibility. I cannot change the cards I was dealt. What I can do is decide how to play my hand.

I am positive there will be times in the future where I have a severe episode and my condition will take over, but that does not stop me from trying to prevent this.

The more severe episodes we have, the more damaged our mental health and our lives become. Our goal should be to prevent this from happening. There are no guarantees, but for me, these techniques are working.

We owe it to ourselves to try and be the best we can be, and we certainly owe it to those around us. I am convinced that my husband deals so well with my condition not just because he loves me, but because he sees that I take responsibility and do all I can to stay well.

In the course of my journey with bipolar disorder, I have met many other sufferers. I have complete respect for their experiences as I cannot imagine them – I can only empathise using my own frame of reference. Sadly, I have come across some people who have almost given up; who have accepted the limited time they spend with mental health professionals as the only form of treatment. They have left the rest in the lap of the gods.

This saddens me, as they have not been made aware of the many self-managing techniques out there and the preventative measures they can explore. For some, this is not possible as they are so severely affected that strong medication is the only route – their lives have quite literally been ruined by this cruel condition. Others do not have the blessing of insight or let up from a constant rapid cycling of moods, so constant that there is no time for insight or to catch their breath. But for many of us, there is light at the end of the tunnel: there is a chance for acceptance, understanding, change and responsibility. Since I took this approach, I have never looked back.

I have not eradicated my condition or its effects, but I have taken measures to be the best I can be and been open to trying new things, gaining knowledge and being willing to fail in the hope I may, in some areas, succeed.

The worst has already happened; you have probably experienced, on several occasions, a torturous mental hell most people are fortunate to avoid. You have got this condition, and you have it for life. I have come to learn that from here, the only way is up. Positivity and responsibility are not luck: they are something you actively embrace and choose to let into your life. They are not a miracle gift; they are things that you decide will lead your life and your thoughts. They are something you may not naturally gravitate to and something you will veer away from. Just know when you are veering away and steer yourself back in.

I have known many people who say everything is part of God's plan or fate or that it is meant to be. For many, this brings comfort. My only warning for this would be that it takes the power away from you. You have the power to change your thoughts and actions. You do not have the power to get rid of this condition, but inside you is the power to manage your relationship with it. I have seen many people go through life unhappy with the belief that this was meant to be.

I recently spent time with someone who moans about things but takes no action to change the status quo; who firmly believes if it is meant for you, it will happen. I suggest you speak to successful business leaders, top athletes and anyone who has overcome adversity and try telling them that it was all fate and it just happened. They would rightly be annoyed with you, because it takes away the credit for any of their hard work, effort, sacrifice, risk and positivity. It implies they had no power, no choice and no responsibility for what it is they have achieved.

Top Tips and Key Action Points:

- Accept that this is the hand you have been dealt. You will need to do it in your own time, but coming to a place of acceptance and knowledge will naturally lead you to positivity and responsibility and in turn, to positive action.
- Do not let others dissuade you from finding out more about what you can do.
- Always challenge yourself. This does not mean stressing yourself into another episode. What is does mean is you can start to look at what you can change.
- Bring your learning to life: start implementing what you have learned into practical changes to your life and your outlook.

CHAPTER TEN

Stigma

Over the years, I have observed that the sympathy a broken wrist elicits over a permanent and enduring mental illness like bipolar disorder is amazing. If you have not experienced mental illness, it must be hard to understand or imagine. But we can all imagine the pain of a broken wrist and the support someone with a broken wrist may need. People cannot imagine mental illness as they can't see it. They most likely already have a preconceived idea of the mentally ill.

Historically, the media, be it the news, movies or books, may have portrayed the mentally ill as dangerous, mad or tortured geniuses. Sometimes the lazy language used to describe people whose behaviours we don't immediately understand can fall into the categories of mad, schizo, psycho, crazy and so on. All these words are rooted in the messages society has given us, over the centuries, regarding the mentally ill. Those around you have grown up listening to these messages, which imply any number of things. Many people who have been exposed to these messages can treat mental illness with fear, suspicion and denial.

Society is starting to catch up to some extent: we have seen storylines in popular shows about bipolar disorder, celebrities have spoken out about their experiences and laws are in place to protect the rights of the mentally ill. However, an unfortunate by product of some media coverage is how it has possibly glamourised mental illness. Messages out there celebrate bipolar disorder as the root of the creative genius and some people are looking back and posthumously diagnosing deceased famous and influential figures. These people may well have had the condition and the more modern treatments were not available for them, which is saddening.

Some extremely talented, creative and intellectual individuals have bipolar disorder and we should, of course, shine a spotlight on these people, if they are willing. It shows society that many people with bipolar disorder contribute positively to the world and are not to be feared. But is society fully accepting of 'average Joe' and his bipolar disorder? I have noticed in my work with people with addiction that if they are poor, from the wrong side of the tracks or not highly educated, then there can be a certain attitude towards them, yet we fully support the celebrity who comes out about their 'addiction hell'. If we are to embrace mental illness, then we need to embrace it all; from bestselling authors and musicians to those who are unemployed and homeless, and where appropriate, society needs to fully support adequate access to the right support services.

Of course, any dialogue and exposure around bipolar disorder is positive. It puts it into mainstream society to be discussed, debated and acknowledged. I would not stop it becoming part of mainstream culture; we have been hidden away for too long.

My discussions with some mental health professionals have highlighted that more people are getting diagnosed with bipolar disorder. This is a good thing, as from diagnosis, people can start to treat, manage and recover. The unfortunate side effect is that people who do not have bipolar disorder could be seeking a diagnosis. This is dangerous not only for those people, but for those who are truly suffering.

People may be saying they have been depressed or high when really they are just experiencing feelings on the normal spectrum of human emotion. The difficulty lies in the diagnosis as there is no blood test or scan that can diagnose, the result being that psychiatrists rely on what people say about their moods and also how they may present at a hospital or clinic. I cannot understand why anyone who does not have this condition would want to be diagnosed with it as there is just so much stigma and pain still related to it.

The increased awareness of bipolar disorder in society is wonderful. However, I have come across people who start to try and diagnose those around them. Where someone is a bit moody or grumpy, people say they think that person must have bipolar disorder, when in fact that person is just moody, grumpy and poor company. What is still lacking is a fundamental understanding of the condition. Society needs a greater understanding of the severity of the condition and the terrifying experiences of sufferers.

My thoughts in this chapter may be controversial and I know this as I write. However, this should not be interpreted as an opinion against diagnosis or seeking treatment. If even one person gets the correct diagnosis and the right help following media exposure of bipolar disorder, then that is a wonderful thing. If someone has the confidence to speak out and ask for help as a result of media coverage, then that should be celebrated. My only concern is that if people are demanding a diagnosis for whatever reason, where a diagnosis should not be, it damages the mental health movement as a whole and those living with bipolar disorder. It absolutely plays into the hands of the doubters who see a diagnosis of mental illness as weak, sponging off the state, all in someone's head or as a trendy addition to the 21st century.

I am also strongly in favour of positive role models in the media and if famous people speak out, we should admire their courage and celebrate their exposure. My concern again is that some are not role models. As a society, we have become increasingly fixated on seeing people have meltdowns or discuss their personal issues on international television and often this is not done for the purpose of education, awareness raising and reducing stigma, but for entertainment and titillation.

Maybe there is something in society today that makes some people feel better about their own lives when someone else's is clearly a mess. What we need are real, genuine and frank role models and messages. Famous people should absolutely do this as they have the advantage of being respected and in the public eye, and I am eternally grateful for the documentary, about bipolar disorder, that Stephen Fry[4] took part in as it helped educate those around me and generated discussion. Colleagues and relatives explained how, after watching it, they felt they had a better understanding of bipolar disorder and had previously misunderstood its severity.

Mental illness, like many disabilities and conditions, is not always pretty. But mental illness is in all walks of life and in all communities and we need to look at it, even if it if makes us uncomfortable. Sufferers do need to have the confidence to speak out so as a society, as communities and as human beings, we can reduce stigma and tackle misconceptions head on.

Positive role models are essential in showing the newly diagnosed that bipolar disorder need not be an automatic barrier to success, achievement or leading a full and rewarding life. What we need now is for others to catch up and accept this. As sufferers of bipolar disorder, we should also recognise that the illness does create barriers. It may be societal barriers; it may be our own, but we would, as our own bipolar life coaches, be naïve if we were to think we could carry on as normal and face no barriers.

I know that my mission to remain well, managed and healthy has affected my career. There have been certain promotions I have avoided due to the increased stress levels. This is not negativity; this is positivity, as I know my triggers and my condition. This does not mean I have given up. What it has meant for me is that I am increasingly seeking new ways to challenge myself, channel my talents and achieve a healthy bipolar disorder work-life balance. Training as a life coach has enabled me to use the skills and talents I have to help others. What I want to stress here, however, is that there are and will be barriers that your condition places on you and that others and society places on you – know the difference.

I was once asked in a job interview if my having Bipolar disorder meant I could have an 'attack' at work. I suspect in some job interviews, I really was the best candidate on the day, but my bipolar disorder prevented a job offer. This is, of course, illegal, but the law is an ass and there are always ways around it. I have struggled to get life insurance, practically had to beg for a driving licence and have been paid lip service by many people who just wanted to be politically correct and then get the hell away from me!

Do not misunderstand me – I do not think everyone and everything should bend over backwards to accommodate me. I do not think the world owes me a living. However, what I am owed is respect, inclusion, equal rights and acceptance. We are not there yet, but as our own bipolar life coaches, we owe it to ourselves and to others with the condition to be the best we can be; to be role models and champions and to play our hand the best we can.

I have described before the feeling of being a square peg in a world of round holes, and most days I do feel this way. I have worked myself into the ground in the past to prove I deserved my job; that I was as valuable as anyone else and to prove that I was no different. On reflection, this was not always the best approach, as I made myself ill by creating so much additional stress. I am different and on occasion I will need an employer or those around me to make 'reasonable adjustments'.

I have often been so busy trying to fit in and prove myself that I have denied who I really am. I have been so terrified of being a stereotype that I have enforced some of society's prejudices upon myself. I have been so desperate to prove I am just the same as everyone else and have denied my true identity. The joke has been on me.

So as I have come to accept my condition, I have also come to accept that there will be times when I need support in order to prevent becoming unwell. This is OK. This is who I am. My opinion is the one that matters and I think I am valuable, relevant and doing well.

So what does this all have to do with stigma? Firstly, do not impose stigma on yourself. If you don't believe in yourself, how will others? Some views of the mentally ill are archaic. Accept this and move forward. Your behaviours and positivity will prove the exception to the rule, and you may start to change opinions, one person at a time. You are a trailblazer for future generations with bipolar disorder, and this is both a responsibility and an opportunity.

Understand that negative views of the mentally ill are sometimes deeply entrenched and this is the point that some people are starting from. You do not have to accept this, but you do need to understand it. Without understanding, there can be no change. You will not change everyone's opinion, just like you will never change my husband's choice of football club: this allegiance has been indoctrinated in him from childhood.

Any change or any progress regarding mental illness is good, but you will not always feel understood and accepted. To spend your entire life railing against this each and every time you experience stigma will wear you out. Choose your battles and hold your head up high. This is the groundwork you need to do before broaching our next chapter, which is about telling family and friends and also managing your relationships with them.

Top Tips and Key Action Points:

- Understand where people's views are coming from – they may not be a personal attack but rooted in traditional views, fear and ignorance.
- Understand that no matter how much information someone is given, they may not change their minds.
- Seek positive role models for bipolar disorder and seek to be one.
- You may want to challenge stigma in an organised and positive way, such as supporting a mental health charity.
- Understand what are your barriers and what are someone else's – you only have the power to work on your own

- If people ask questions following media exposure of mental illness, answer honestly (as much as you are comfortable with). Any discussion is good.
- Celebrate your individuality.
- Stigma is fact. Accept this and do not let it destroy you. Prove people wrong, challenge it and contribute to change, but do not let it fuel internal anger – it only damages you.

CHAPTER ELEVEN

Family and Friends

This chapter has been one of the hardest to write. I may offend loved ones, and I am sorry, but again, it is important to share common experiences in order to support the reader.

In the years before my diagnosis, I had experienced strange behaviours, highs and lows. I relied on family and friends for support. However, my moods must have been frustrating and confusing for them. I didn't know what was going on, so why the hell should they? Mentally, I had been in a very unhappy place for some time, interspersed with some fantastic and frightening manias. This was due to my undiagnosed mood disorder.

My mother spent hours with me on the phone, as did friends. My torment was probably bewildering to them and must have caused worry. I am grateful for the support they offered and the time they spent. However, I do remember other family members and friends becoming increasingly frustrated with me. Why could I not just pull myself together and stop complaining? Because I was severely depressed or manic.

Upon diagnosis, I was terrified of telling my parents and terrified of telling friends. Would they still love me and accept me? I was so worried that eventually hospital medical staff intervened and invited my parents to a meeting where we could tell them more. In the end it went OK. I think my parents were shell-shocked and obviously worried about my future. I remember them asking questions about how well tested my medication had been when what I think I needed was someone to hold me and tell me it was going to be OK. But how could they? No one knew it was going to be OK. Some friends were great whilst others reduced and eventually ceased contact. This was disappointing, but not surprising.

As I forged ahead and educated myself, I wanted those around me to learn more, and I do think this is a useful approach. However, people are busy and so may not always have time to learn more. I set about trying to educate people. I gave out books, leaflets, and my thoughts. Some people took it on board, and others didn't really try. This is their choice and I respect that. However, although I am no one else's responsibility and it is down to me to manage my condition, earn a living and care for myself, I do sometimes feel that I need those around me to have a good understanding of what I need. There will be times as with any severe and enduring illness that I will need additional support, be it emotional or 24-hour care. I need my husband with me most nights due the effects of my evening medication.

A few years ago I broke my finger in an accident and had an operation. This was of course painful, distressing and inconvenient. The outpouring of sympathy, offers of help, understanding and empathy for my 'plight' was astounding. I felt like a celebrity. When I have an episode, many people go quiet. They may think I need time alone and respectfully keep their distance, but what many never do is ask what they can do or what I need. This small yet significant question would mean the world to me.

Sometimes an offer of a visit, a phone call where I am not expected to behave in any particular way or the odd text can make a real difference in combating the feelings of isolation. Many do this and again they know what I need and so phone, text and meet, but what they don't do is put pressure on me. Knowing I have company and contact with the outside world is also a comfort to my husband. Others just can't handle it or try but handle it badly.

This is not written to garner feelings of pity. It is written to set the scene for you and your journey towards managing your relationship with bipolar disorder and your relationships with those around you.

Probably like me, you will experience feelings of anger, denial and doom after diagnosis, peppered with relief. It will take time for you to get your head around it. Therefore, offer those around you the courtesy of getting their heads around it, too. It will take them time. Manage people's expectations. Mental health professionals frequently tell me that there are common questions families and loved ones have about bipolar disorder. These tend to be, "When will they be better?", "Why are they like this?" and "Why can't they just pull themselves together?"

In short, there are no definitive answers to these questions, although the glaringly obvious one of when will they be better can be answered in the briefest of ways with the word "never". This does not mean you will not have a rewarding life and not experience periods of stability. What is does mean is there is no cure and you have this for life.

Loved ones need to be told this. Pretending will not alter this fact and will only complicate things in the future. Following a recent episode, someone said they were disappointed this condition kept coming back. I had to again point out it never goes away and if they could not get their head around this, they would be constantly disappointed. I can do no more in this case. I have been honest, there will be no miracle cure and words such as "disappointed" do not help me.

I am also aware of the guilt that some people can place on me, albeit unconsciously. They want answers as to when I will be better, are very upset if I have to cancel a prior engagement, and are disappointed if I have to take time off work, and this can stoke the fire of depression, feeding into the hateful feelings I can have about myself. You will more than likely experience a similar thing with some people in your life.

I used to let these reactions upset me, which then fed directly into my depression. It was all the evidence and proof I needed that I was useless and a failure – that is, until I became my own bipolar life coach and realised the only person that could make me feel a failure was me! I am happy with my decisions: they are measured, responsible and generally made with the aim of remaining well. I could choose whether to let those messages in and affect me or I could reject them, safe in the knowledge that I am doing fine.

I have some friends, relatives and even colleagues who tell me how proud they are of me and the way I manage my condition. They say my strength to tackle this head on and manage it so well is amazing. This acknowledgement and encouragement is a real tonic – it spurs me on and makes me feel less alone. I also receive messages at the other end of the scale. My attitude now is that you can't win 'em all! But I now have the strength to recognise this and the power to reject certain messages and move forward.

So what does all this mean for you? Firstly, I want to say I *understand*. The above should all be evidence of this. You are not alone if you are finding it hard to sustain relationships, get the right support and be surrounded by people who genuinely get it. My previous chapter on stigma highlighted that attitudes to mental illness are instilled in many from birth. People cannot see it and this makes it hard for them to understand. Images they have seen in the past of the mentally ill may have created fear, and the distance to understanding may be vast. Some cultures, be they based in religion, societal or even family cultures, cannot accept mental illness and for some, this means that your condition will never be OK. For others, there is hope.

Start to communicate with loved ones. Tell them about the condition and get support from mental health professionals with this. Some people may find it easier to read information leaflets, whereas others will need to communicate face to face. Let loved ones ask questions. I have been asked what could be deemed as prejudiced or offensive questions by people, but this was not my focus. My focus was that this person wanted to know more, learn and help. Making people feel comfortable to ask questions no matter how badly worded will keep dialogue open. Educating loved ones is also essential as they may see the signs of elevated or low mood before you do. Those closest to you can see changes as they get to know your condition and triggers better. I have what I call my inner circle. This is a small group of people that includes my husband and some dear friends who have fantastic knowledge and insight into my condition. They have been told not to be scared of challenging me where necessary. One friend is particularly good at subtly suggesting I take a break or questioning whether I am doing too much. I know her and she knows me and in the past, has seen things before I did and was annoyingly always right!

I have a wonderful group of friends who accept me as I am and who are accepting of my bipolar disorder. They also never put pressure on me and are used to being cancelled at short notice. They know I won't drink, stay out late and so on and respect this. They do not find my condition boring or limiting as we work around it. Their encouragement and support humbles me and I hope I am as good a friend to them as they are to me. They are great at letting me decide what we do. Sometimes I prefer to see them in my home and there are times when we plan things and I cannot face it, such as shopping in a big crowd. They let me alter our plans without complaint. I have done a good job in educating them, but they have also educated themselves, observed and listened. They treat me the same as anyone else and therefore do not make me feel different or demanding. At the same time, they appreciate that at times, we will need to make reasonable adjustments to accommodate my condition.

My husband has educated himself and allowed me to educate him. I had been diagnosed for a while before we met and so was able to educate him from the word go. He was never under any illusions that I am anything other than what I am. I did not sugar coat it for him, as he had to know what he was getting into.

Living with someone who has bipolar disorder is not easy. It must be so hard to watch your spouse go through an episode and it must also be terrible to have the knowledge that at some point your spouse may not be in full control of their behaviour. Suicide must hover like an unspoken threat. As much as I am always watching my moods, so is he. He must be as paranoid as I am: what does this mood mean, is this feeling telling us something?

He has always allowed me to tell him what I need. He is used to the last-minute cancellations of social events, the medicated early nights and the swinging moods that lead to an episode. He is OK with the slightly regimented life I live in order to stay well, but is also not afraid to intervene when he needs to. He knows that not only is he married to me, he is also married to bipolar disorder.

Whatever my mood, he is there, and his love, dedication and patience are a constant guiding light on the mainland as I battle through stormy seas. He is my hero.

What does this mean for you? There will be people in your life who want to know more, help more and support more. Let them. Don't allow yourself to be smothered, as this is not healthy and does not lead to sensible self-management. But let people in. Some people will disappoint you and some will amaze you with their kindness and insight.

Allow those around you to make mistakes – none of us are perfect. Put yourself in their position: they cannot see physical symptoms, this condition is alien to them; they may be upset and scared or even in denial. It is frightening to see someone's moods change and their behaviour and thoughts become destructive or strange. But do not feel that you should not say anything where something has been damaging or is not working for you.

There are people who think by just sheer force of encouragement and getting on with it, I will be OK and will avoid an episode. This is based in love and not wanting me to be ill, but is naïve. I now have the confidence to know what works for me and no amount of encouragement or glossing over the issue will change that. If others see you as weak for addressing your feelings or dealing properly with an episode, let them. Remember that by addressing things, you are demonstrating courage, insight and responsibility. Also remember what signifies strength and well-being to others may not be what works for you. I know that if

I focus on minutiae and direct my stress in the wrong ways, it will not be beneficial for me. I know that if I don't maintain a dialogue with bipolar disorder and respect it, it will destroy me.

It is ironic that I am about to write the following given that I am giving advice in this book, but beware of advice. Advice can be well meaning but wrong, and it can also be a veiled attempt at control and manipulation. Listen to advice by all means, but learn what suits you. Some advice will be fantastic and life-changing and so be open to suggestions, but do not follow it purely to meet the needs of others. Beware of hidden agendas and misguided opinions wrapped up in advice. Your condition will be inconvenient to others. It will mess up social plans and it may even mean you have to miss important events. Never use this as a tool to manipulate everything to be the way you want it to be, but do make others aware that sometimes an episode or early warning sign will take precedence.

You don't need to constantly go on about your condition and never, ever use it as a bargaining tool or to pour guilt on someone; this is manipulation. However, you do need to make it clear to those in your life that it is an important part of who you are.

In the previous chapter, I encouraged you to be a trailblazer and to change opinion one person at a time. Allow those around you to see the efforts you are making to remain well. Let them see your determination and positivity as this can contribute to mutual respect. If others can see you doing everything you can, being responsible and taking the appropriate steps to remain well, they will hopefully follow with support and love.

There will be people who will not be able to accept and understand or who simply don't want to. Keep working at these relationships, but it is also OK to reach a place where you can no longer maintain them. This is a very personal decision and the effects can be upsetting and affect others in the wider family, so I am not going to advise on this. It has to be up to you.

I have come to a point in my life where I am more selective about whom I let in and whom I confide in. I have been hurt too many times and also constantly felt like a disappointment and for me, this is no longer acceptable. I don't know if this signifies maturity, wisdom, weariness, or stubbornness, but what I do know is that it has decreased my feelings of stress and frustration.

Top Tips and Key Action Points:

- Pick your time to tell people and don't always let their first reaction be the one that stays with you. They may be shocked, scared, angry and confused, so allow people the courtesy to express these emotions – they, like you, will need time to come to terms with this.
- Keep dialogue open and allow people to ask questions. They may not be phrased well, but it does signify that they want to learn more, and this is a good thing.
- Source information for others, or at least direct them to it.

- Include your medical team where appropriate. They may be able to answer any questions that loved ones may have.
- Understand where stigma and fear come from and work with others to help them overcome this.
- Allow people to see your struggles and triumphs. They can learn more this way and hopefully see your positivity.
- Accept you may lose some relationships – this is not about you. I lost some friendships, but what I came to learn was this opened up new possibilities and meant I had more time for the wonderful friendships that developed along the way.
- Tell people what you need – no one is a mind reader.
- Accept people will do things that are not helpful but are well-intentioned. The test is when you ask someone to change this or do it differently. Gauge the reaction to your request: if someone is genuine, they will want to adapt certain things and learn what to do for the best.
- Have empathy for those around you. Bear in mind that this is not easy for them.
- Learn what support feels like for you and let in those who can provide it.
- Let people know what language is helpful. You do not want to be patronised, but some language is more helpful than others: "weak", "disappointed", "upset", "worried", "should" and "ought to" are rarely helpful.
- Remember you are your own bipolar life coach. There will always be some things, some people and some opinions you cannot change, but what you can change is your reaction to them.

CHAPTER TWELVE

Communication with others

So far, we have looked at positive thinking, changing your mind set, being your own bipolar life coach, and relationships. Communication is what can bring all these elements together for the better. We have considered changing the way we communicate with ourselves to lead towards a healthy inner life and a different outlook. Communication used in the right way can be a powerful tool in bettering and managing your relationships with others.

The best time to start to change the way you communicate will be when you are experiencing a relatively stable mood. If you start practising when you are well, it will soon start to become more natural.

Communicating a message to bring about change, increase dialogue, and influence others is a powerful tool. As stated previously, do not use your condition to manipulate others, but do have the confidence to ask or suggest what others can do to support you.

The first step to better communication with others is ensuring that you know what you want to say. What is your message? Are you asking for something? Are you challenging someone? Are you hoping to bring about change? Know what you want to achieve. It may help to write it down to gain greater clarity. Make notes on the situations that this will improve or prevent.

Once you are on message, pick your time and place. This does not need to be perfect, and for some things, there is never a right time, but choose wisely. Is having a conversation about a sensitive issue with your close friend best done when she has been up all night with her baby? Similarly, is e-mail the best way to do something, or is it better face to face? Think this through.

The environment is important and a neutral venue may be more appropriate. In your home, the recipient could feel ambushed, and in theirs, you may feel it is disrespectful to challenge them.

Stay on message. You have come this far; so do not lose your nerve at the crucial moment. Remind yourself why you are doing this. It is a positive thing to improve relations and reduce the risk of future conflict and is for your long-term benefit. We are often not good at asking for what we want or requesting a change, and for many of us it is an alien concept. If you feel you are backtracking or losing your courage, take a moment to imagine the outcome you want and think about how much happier you and others may be if it is achieved.

Be sensitive to your recipient. You need to keep them engaged and on side. Starting off with a criticism or an accusing tone will immediately put the recipient into a position of defence, and their natural instinct may be to fight back, or at least, to not listen properly. Do not accuse, using phrases like, "You make me feel useless when you keep asking when I am going back to work"; of course the recipient will be offended.

Instead, try a phrase such as, "It is great that you care so much and I can understand you may be keen for me to get back to work, but sometimes I can feel pressure from this and so it would be helpful if I could tell you when I am ready in my own time". Immediately, you have started off with a positive and have made this about the way you feel, rather than the recipient being the root of bad feeling – you have avoided blame. In an ideal world, this would be enough, but I know from my own experience that resentment and denial can run deep, and so you may need to have several attempts at this before your point is clear and change is brought about.

This type of conversation may not come naturally to you, and so you may need some practice. Try out different ways of saying things. It could be in front of a mirror, with a trusted friend or mental health professional. Once you start to feel comfortable with the words and the way you feel, it will be easier to do in practice. You will feel more confident and assured. Do not be a victim. You need to feel you deserve a better outcome – we all have relationships where we fall into old behaviours where one person is more dominant, and we certainly can all identify with turning into a stroppy teenager when dealing with our parents. So stop, breathe, and again, remember what you want to achieve.

I recently had to bring about change with loved ones. I had always felt that my episodes were a disappointment and inconvenience, and that I was always being asked the same questions. These were questions that the people asking thought would elicit information that would prove I was well, unwell, making progress or not, and in fairness, were rooted fully in concern and love. I felt these questions were not helpful, and produced feelings of guilt and signified pressure. This may have been purely my interpretation, but such conversations had remained the same for years, and in the end, resulted in my feeling bad.

I decided that for everyone's benefit, I needed to make an intervention. I explained that these questions were not helpful and that really they didn't signify anything. I also was able to explain that I was doing well with regards to managing my condition and that to not manage it well could have dire consequences. I explained that it was not helpful at certain times to feel pressure and that it would be really helpful for me to be surrounded by people offering the right kind of support.

Unfortunately, a common theme for people with bipolar disorder is that others do not accept it. Loved ones are frustrated and cannot see your condition. If you were limping because of a broken knee, they could offer to help you out of a chair, carry your shopping and do any number of practical tasks. With mental illness, many do not know what to do.

Below is a scenario that may give you an example of how communicating in the right way can bring about change.

Sadie has bipolar disorder, and when she is experiencing the feelings of a depression coming, she starts to put things in place to try and manage this. Sadie's brother has had trouble accepting her depressive episodes. Sadie has a family party coming up that she knows she will not want to attend – not because she is giving in to her condition, but because she knows that she needs to take a few days out to rest and recuperate. Sadie tells her brother she cannot go to the family party, and her brother becomes angry and says he had hoped she would have the strength to go. He says he is bitterly disappointed and that her nieces will be devastated. In the past, Sadie would have taken on board the upset and guilt through the emotive language used and may have started an argument through feeling criticised. However, Sadie now recognises this for what it is.

Sadie wants to keep relations strong with her family but needs to communicate the message that her brother's behaviour is not helpful. Sadie allows her brother his anger and politely says she is not feeling too good and so must come off the phone. A day or so later, having talked it through with a friend, Sadie calls her brother and asks if they can meet for coffee. Sadie hugs him as normal and asks after her sister-in-law and nieces. When the moment feels right, Sadie wants to shout:

"Why do you have to be so mean to me? You make me feel guilty and I feel like I am always letting you down.

You can't accept my condition; you don't know what this is like. Why are you like this?"

Instead, Sadie pauses, holds up her red flag and recalls the conversation she ran through with her friend, and says instead:

"It is lovely to see you – thanks for taking the time to meet up. I am sorry I had to miss the party. I was disappointed to miss out, as I would have loved to be part of the celebrations. This condition can be limiting and frustrating for me, so I can understand your frustration. I do not want to let you down, but I also need to do all I can to stay well. This is a serious condition and I am doing a good job of managing it. Unfortunately, there will be times when it gets in the way, just like any condition. If you had the flu, I would be disappointed you could not come to my social event, as I enjoy your company, but would understand that you had to put your health first.

"I know you care about me and it is great to feel my company is wanted, but if I feel someone is angry with me, it can slow down my recovery. I am quite sensitive when I am feeling low, and so feeling like I have disappointed or made someone angry is very upsetting for me. I do not want to feel guilty and find it helpful when those around me are understanding and trust my judgement as, overall, I am managing well. It is always nice to know my company will be missed, but it would be lovely if you could say this instead of other things."

Sadie has challenged her brother politely and has requested change in a non-confrontational way. Her brother now has the information she needed him to have. He may not immediately respond, but with gentle reminders, may start to change his behaviour. Sadie will see over time whether her language has had an effect. However, after a number of times with no change, Sadie will need to alter her mind set, accept her brother is not capable of change and reject his messages or move on.

Using communication to bring about change is something we can all do. Observe the experienced retail manager dealing with a disgruntled customer. They adopt a tone they hope will calm the customer down and hope that the customer will eventually start to mirror this. They are representing a retail brand and so cannot lose their temper; make it personal or storm off. If they did, they may find themselves in hot water.

My work in coaching and advice and guidance is all based on communication: communicating in a certain way to gather information about the client, guiding a discussion with a client, listening patiently and so on. This is my professional life and I do it well. But I am far from perfect. I can at times find it hard to hide my frustrations in work and in my personal life. We are all fallible, but recognising where we are falling into bad habits is essential.

In my personal life, I can easily fall into the trap of old behaviours, old resentments and familiar arguments, especially with family. Does this make me ill-equipped to be my own bipolar life coach? No – it means I am human and not perfect. But now what I can do is recognise when this is happening and address it. There is always scope for improvement, and this is why I find my work so interesting. Never give up trying to improve, learn more and achieve. I think the day I stop being curious about life, people, psychology, relationships, communication and what it means to be alive and to be human is the day I will draw my last breath.

Top Tips and Key Action Points:

- Communication and language can be powerful. Use this to improve your relationships, not to point a finger or manipulate.
- Reflect on how you would wish to be spoken to and treated – it may be an old cliché, but is a really useful barometer.
- Accept that you cannot change everyone and everything to suit you and your needs.
- Choose which issues are causing you the most upset and start to think how you can respectfully and lovingly bring about change.
- Timing is everything – choose this well.
- Environment is important – neutral is best.
- What is your message? Be clear about this.
- Practice what you are going to say beforehand. Feel the words in your mouth and your head and be comfortable with them.
- Stay on message and don't lose your nerve.
- Start with a positive.
- Don't accuse and avoid language rooted in blame: "You make me feel...."

- If you mess up, try again in the future – do not give up.
- Remember, not everyone will welcome what you have to say, and in some cases, you will need to let it go and change your reaction to it to protect yourself – you may need to rethink how you communicate with this person in the future.
- Do not try to bring about change in an argument – it will not happen. Avoid words of hurt, walk away and come back to it.

CHAPTER THIRTEEN

Lifestyle

Being your own bipolar life coach, we have come to discover, is about managing, responsibility, education and taking control. So it makes sense that there are many changes you can make to your lifestyle that may be beneficial. Respect your condition, manage your relationship with it and take appropriate steps to do all you can to make the most of things.

This chapter is broken into subheadings, and I have tried to keep it simple. If you're not there yet in terms of accepting your condition, feeling positive about it, engaging in talking therapies or changing your inner life and relationships with others, the information below will be a starting point. These are small changes we can all make to improve our life and our relationship with bipolar disorder.

Timetable Your Life

This may sound ridiculous, but it is an effective tool for many with bipolar disorder. Modern life can put many demands on our time and energy. There is often always something to do. If we reflect on our triggers, stressors and build-up to an episode, then the next logical thing after a mood diary is to plan our lives. This does not need to be with military precision and, as discussed previously, life can throw up unexpected challenges. You cannot control everything, but you can try to manage your life so that your condition and staying well remains your priority.

Look honestly and objectively at your life and your lifestyle. Work out what is a priority. Soulless as it may seem, work is one of my priorities. This is because I have to work to pay the bills and because I enjoy working. Work provides me with a social, creative, and intellectual outlet. Work can be beneficial for my self-esteem and independence. If I am unwell, I can't work, full stop, and am of no use to my clients. Therefore, I plan around my work pattern. This does not mean that I never have to take time off, but it does mean that the likelihood of this is reduced.

Timetabling can be achieved with a sensible approach. Sticking to a sleep pattern is important, as is predicting how demanding my work schedule will be in a given week or period. A teacher may find the run-up to exam season particularly stressful; an accountant the approach to the end of the financial year, and the retail assistant the run up to Christmas. Start to anticipate significant periods of stress and plan for this: reduce your social commitments, get help with the children, physically plan in time to relax, and stick to a healthy sleep pattern.

There will be times when no matter how well you have planned things, life will throw up something new to deal with. Never just keep adding to your stress. Take a look at your timetable and work out what can go in order to deal with the new challenge. Be in tune to what and how you are feeling. You may have to cancel one commitment to deal with another. We are not superhuman and we have bipolar disorder. It will not go away and when you don't respect it, it will come for you!

I am very lucky in my friendships and my friends are used to being cancelled and rearranged. Such friends are true friends and the ones who did not accept this are sadly no longer in my life. My friends know I love them and love to spend time with them, but they also understand the power of my condition and the consequences of not managing it.

My husband is used to going solo at social events. He knows that when I am feeling stressed or close to an episode, there are commitments I have to pull back from. He never complains and never pressures me. My husband is also used to leaving events earlier than others and to getting to bed at a sensible time, even on holiday.

Not everyone is as lucky as I am in their friendship groups and relationships. Continue to educate those around you, using non-confrontational and supportive language. Try and establish ground rules and agreements when you are stable – and never in anger. Remember you can choose who you let into your life. This is all an important part of being able to timetable your life and being able to identify what can go at certain times.

Saying No

This is an important element of timetabling your life and possibly one of the greatest things you can do for your mental health. Saying no does not mean withdrawing from life and living a boring existence – nor should it be manipulated just to get out of things you don't want to do or don't like. However, being able to say no, or at least maybe, rather than yes, is something you need to make peace with. Are you a pleaser? Many of us are, and this forces us into situations where we can put other people's feelings ahead of our health. I was once one of these people and have had to work on my ability to say no.

Many assertiveness courses focus on being able to say no, so take comfort in the fact that you are not alone if you are finding this difficult. It is not always an easy thing to do, as we may feel guilty or uncomfortable. First of all, revisit your thought processes, especially if you are prone to always agreeing to things no matter how much they may affect your health. When you are about to agree to something you know is going to be bad for your mental health, recognise it, pause, hold up your red flag, and redirect your thoughts into saying no. Refer back to the chapter on communication: you are less likely to cause offence by choosing your words carefully and by not reflecting guilt or blame.

Exercise

You may be on strong medication, feeling low or generally lethargic, and exercise is probably the last thing on your mind. It was for me. But I have found exercise to be life-changing. It can contribute to the release of feel good chemicals, improve sleep, and in most cases, contributes to overall physical and mental health, manages weight and makes you feel *good*!

I cannot stress enough how important exercise is to managing my condition and staying well. Of course, there are days when I don't feel like it, but if I push on through, the difference is amazing. Not only can exercise provide physical benefits, it can also provide you with that all-important time to yourself. I remember one mental health practitioner telling me they could not be bothered with exercise and didn't know why I did it. I find this shocking and again, question their knowledge. Your mental health team may well not mention exercise, as their time is limited. This is another reason I wanted to write this.

What type of exercise to try is a personal decision. You should consult your doctor, as there may be some exercise you need to avoid because of medication effects or other physical complaints. But once you have cleared this, find out what works for you. A brisk walk in the sunshine or a strong wind can be great for clearing the head, and of course is free. Find a setting that works for you. Joining a gym may be better for you, as there are a variety of machines and weights and you will be able to have a custom-made fitness programme designed. Depending on the facility, gym membership can also have other benefits, such as saunas, steam rooms and hot tubs, which can be excellent for relaxation. You may wish to join fitness classes where you are given structured direction. This way, you are more likely to complete your workout. Classes can also be a way to meet people and reduce feelings of isolation, especially if you are unable to work.

You may not feel able to tackle full on cardiovascular exercise and want something more gentle and therapeutic. Yoga and Pilates are examples of exercise I undertake to support my physical health, but also my mental health. Even during an episode, I try to embrace exercise, especially on the days when I am tempted to lie in the dark. With exercise, I can go to the gym, not speak to anyone, put in my earphones, work out and blend into the background. Exercise reminds me that I am alive and can kick-start feel-good chemicals that lead to a more positive outlook. It is important, however, to monitor your approach to exercise. Are you over-exercising? Do you have more energy for it than usual? No matter how much you do, could you do more? This could be an indicator that you are entering a manic phase.

Healthy Eating

A healthy balanced diet should complement any exercise regime. This does not mean life should be miserable with no treats. I find cooking and baking for others therapeutic and so do have treats. But as with any health condition, maintaining a healthy diet is important, as it can help reduce the risk of other health complications. Some people find certain medications can influence their weight, and so following a healthy diet can be a way of managing this. Eating a healthy diet can reduce the risk of various conditions and also contribute to your body getting the right balance of nutrients.

I have been a smoker in the past and so will not judge anyone who smokes. This is not to say I endorse it or think it has any health benefits, but I have had to challenge myself and my mind set in terms of smoking. I had come to see smoking as a way of helping manage stress; a coping mechanism, when in reality, it has probably been another crutch, like sweet food or alcohol. It is advisable to stop smoking, but choose your time well. You are more likely to succeed if cessation is planned and tackled when you are feeling well. I was once told by a mental health professional that most of her bipolar disorder patients smoked. I am not sure what this signifies. Are we more likely to be addicted to something? Is it helping us cope, or is it just another bad and unhealthy habit that we need to kick?

Remember to live your life well and a good rule is things in moderation. I am not suggesting you exist like a monk. Life is to be enjoyed, experienced and lived. However there are things we can do to support our well-being and overall health.

Sleep

A good night's sleep is essential in managing bipolar disorder. I have quite a strict bedtime routine – not because I am a party pooper, but because this is one thing I can control to help manage my condition. In order to be able to work and stay in the best health, I need a regular sleep pattern. It also means I am better able to manage any side effects from medication.

Try to follow a regular routine with sleep. I know it may sound boring and not what you want to hear, but this is a severe and enduring illness; a disability, and you need to accommodate it. Stick as much as possible to the same sleep and waking times. This will set your body clock.

Of course, there are times when my routine is upset – a special occasion, for example. But most of the time, I don't really deviate. I no longer stay out late clubbing, and although this is also to do with maturity, I am not prepared to unnecessarily upset my routine.

During a manic phase, sleep, as we know, is the last thing we want. But sleep we must. Once I recognise a high, I have an agreement with my psychiatrist where I take additional medication to induce sleep and slow me down. I have yet to find another, more natural approach to getting to sleep during a high. But I am sure it is out there, and I urge you to continue your research. In general, I do not rely on this additional medication to bring about sleep in everyday life. I rely on myself and self-management.

I am almost evangelical about sleep, and my husband knows the minute he is snoring, he is sent to the spare room. It may sound harsh, but he respects what I need to do to stay well. Similarly, laptops, televisions and so on are banned from the bedroom. Having electronic devices in the room is not relaxing. It creates stimulation and is bad "sleep hygiene". One thing I do like to do is read novels before sleep. I find this takes my mind off the events of the day by transporting me into the story and also relaxes me and makes me sleepy. You may find other things work better for you. Try a relaxing bath. Listening to specially produced relaxation music can also help.

If your thoughts are running away with you, consider keeping a note pad by the bed to jot anything down. It may be a negative thought you need to address or a task you are worried about forgetting to do. By writing it down, you will be safe in the knowledge that you can deal with it in the morning.

Another technique I have is to lie in the dark and focus on my breathing, then relaxing every bit of my body one part at a time. This is a technique my mother taught me as a child and has stayed a useful way to concentrate on relaxation.

I am not a parent and so have never faced the horrors of waking to tend to a crying baby or toddler. This of course will happen if you are a parent. It is essential you agree a schedule or tactic to address this with your partner. I have now made a conscious decision not to have a family, as I put my condition first but there was a time when my husband and I were trying for this and we had many discussions about how night times would work, as we knew this was so important to my staying well. If you are a single parent, is there anyone in your life that can help out to give you at least one night of uninterrupted sleep? Can you go to bed at the same time as your child and wake up when they generally do?

Holidays are great for bipolar disorder. They can mean time out from daily life, time to reconnect with loved ones and time to relax. However, be wary of what a time difference, a long-haul flight or even a lot of sun can do. It can interrupt your body clock and sleep pattern.

This is not to say don't go on foreign holidays, but plan your sleep and medication to fit in.

Alcohol and Illicit Drugs

Before my diagnosis, I self-medicated my moods, as I did not know what was happening to me. Having read around my subject there are many examples of people out there who have done the same. Following diagnosis, I drank in moderation, which for many works OK. But as I began to know more about my condition, it became apparent that even this was not worth it. Alcohol and drugs heighten mood and they alter mood. I have enough trouble with my mood and balancing my medication without adding another variable into the mix.

Also, be mindful of your caffeine intake, as this can be damaging during the onset of mania. You are in control of your life and you are responsible for the choices you make – I am not going to preach. However, what I will say, with regards to alcohol, drugs and stimulants, is that you have a mood disorder, and you experience extremes of mood involuntarily. They can destroy your life, your relationships, and your career. Do you really want to add fuel to the fire?

I am not saying that avoiding these things is going to be easy. Remember, drugs are not only damaging, but can get you into legal trouble. For many, drugs are not an issue, as they may not come into your social circle, but alcohol is an acceptable and sociable part of life. We associate alcohol with having a good time, celebrating, letting off steam; all the good things in life. It may be that your friends and family have a social life based around alcohol, and this can make abstinence difficult. I know what it is like to be almost judged for not drinking, being encouraged to just have one or to be called boring. On occasion, I have been treated like a social leper. It is hard to not drink if this has been a large part of your social life and indeed, a past coping mechanism. It is also tedious being sober in a room full of drunken people. They are boring, nowhere near as funny as they think they are and you are not part of the party.

However, over time my social life has shifted, and those friends and family that matter have accepted I do not drink. Over time, I have cultivated my social life to include meeting for a soft drink, a meal, a walk, a day out, etc. At the same time, I do not avoid social events, I just turn them on their head. I can be the driver, I save money and I know I will not be the one with a sore head and embarrassing memories the next day. Hypomanic phases can cause me enough embarrassment without adding drunken exploits to the mix. At first, I missed drinking and what it represented, but I can now honestly say I don't. It helps that I am a confident person and don't need drink to stimulate conversation or talk to people I don't know. I am also not really concerned about what people think of me (a protective shield for my condition and behaviours, maybe) and can get up and dance at a social event without worry.

No mental health professional has ever recommended that I don't drink and many say in moderation, it is fine. This is very much a personal choice. However, do check your medication, as many popular medications for bipolar disorder do not mix well with alcohol. For me, a mood disorder does not mix well with alcohol. Why would I want to magnify or influence severity of mood? Managing my condition has not been easy and has not been without sacrifice, but it has been worth it.

Healthy Alternatives

There are many complementary therapies out there that claim to bring about well-being and cure any number of ailments. Some may work; others may not. Find out what works for you, but never take the advice to cease medication or change treatment from anyone but your mental health team. I have come across alternative healers who have told me that I should stop taking medication as it is of no benefit to me. So be cautious when seeking out alternative therapies. This is not to say they cannot make a wonderful contribution to well-being and self-management. I have found acupuncture to be a great way to relax and clear my mind and also have regular massages and facials; all of which contribute to my overall feeling of well-being and ensure that I take time out for myself.

Shop around with these therapies, as again it is personal choice as to what suits you and also very much depends on your budget.

Guided meditation and visualisation is also a useful tool to calming your thoughts, clearing your mind and gaining clarity. Again, find a reputable practitioner. Of course I am going to say this, but life coaching can also be a fantastic way to plan positively and make changes in your attitude, behaviours, and thought processes, which can lead to a more fulfilling life.

Support Groups

There are support groups out there for people with mental health issues and specifically bipolar disorder. This is a great way of exchanging information and sharing common experiences, and can reduce feelings of isolation. Where you do not have the most supportive people in your life or feel that no one understands, then such groups can be a lifeline. Many support groups allow you to help others and be helped. These environments can be an opportunity to really be yourself, where you don't need to explain your condition.

Find out what groups are in your local area and see if they work for you. When you are feeling more confident, you may want to set up your own, if there is nothing in your local area. Your mental health team can provide information on what is available locally.

Such groups can provide safety, solace and a sense of belonging, especially where there is a co-operative and group-led ethos. However, you must be objective and assess whether this model works for you. Not everyone wants to attend such groups, and so it is a very personal choice as to whether you sustain your attendance.

I am writing about bipolar disorder and also undertake activism work for bipolar disorder-related charities and organisations. However, the group approach did not work for me. In the group I attended, I was made to feel welcome and included. It ran several activities in which I was encouraged to be involved and I met some truly inspiring people who had the same condition as me. However, I did not sustain my attendance. This may seem at odds with my message, but for me, work commitments and other considerations prevented it. But try these things out – it is a personal choice as to whether it suits you.

Work/Study

For many people, work or study constitutes a large part of our life. We can spend more time with colleagues than loved ones during the working week, and so it is important that we give this the acknowledgement it deserves.

Whether to disclose your condition to an employer is a personal decision. For many areas of work, this is a required part of recruitment information and so you have no choice in this. You may find that some areas of work are not open to you due to your condition. Although this may seem unfair, such decisions are now largely based on health and safety and the demands of the job. For many other areas of work, an employer cannot discriminate on the grounds of you having bipolar disorder. The illness is covered by some legislation and therefore a refusal of a job based purely on you having the condition could be challenged.

In the past, I have always disclosed my condition to employers, largely for my own benefit. I did not want secrets, and knew that at times, I may be forced to take time off due to my condition. With my current employer, this has largely worked well, as I am able to highlight where I may be feeling certain triggers and they can put in place "reasonable adjustments" to support me temporarily through a difficult patch. I am fortunate that I work in an industry focused on helping people and therefore many of my colleagues and managers display empathy when any difficulties arise. For many, this is not the case, and in the past, I have experienced stigma and prejudice. This may happen to you. It is important to take a step back and recognise when this is happening and think carefully about what you need to do. Sometimes a union representative can provide support, as can legal professionals and some of the mental health charities.

Discussing your condition with a manager or employer does carry risk. I have heard stories of incredible support and care and have heard others where individuals have been "managed out" due to having bipolar disorder, depression or anxiety. Therefore it has to be a personal decision based on your experiences as to whether you decide to disclose. For me, it has worked well and this can be attributed to employment law, disability discrimination law, my commitment to my work, my honesty and communication and also the open-mindedness of colleagues.

The next thing to consider in terms of work is the suitability of your job or career plans in relation to bipolar disorder. This is part of accepting the condition and the genuine barriers it can create. I do not think that I would be suitable in a job that required night shifts, as this would disrupt my sleep pattern and my medication. I have worked shifts before my diagnosis and looking back, it did contribute to a significant episode. This is not the case for everyone, as we all experience our condition differently, but work out what things are likely to make you unwell and consider such practicalities in relation to your condition and your work.

Meeting your commitments in the workplace is important, as this is related to whether you get paid or sustain your employment. Look out and plan for possible periods of high stress. Is there one particular period coming up that will require you to work additional hours or take on extra work? If so, plan for this, reduce the demands in your personal life, book some leave in between days, make sure you engage in plenty of relaxation and keep your medication and sleep on track. It can be useful to discuss your work patterns and any anticipated periods of stress with your mental health team.

Use your mood diary to identify any issues and use your timetable to look at what can go in this period of additional stress. Use your positive communication to get the support of others. When I am feeling stressed, I lean on my husband to take up more of the household responsibilities such as cooking and cleaning, which is normally shared. This may sound small, but can be an enormous help when I am starting to feel a little overwhelmed. If I am anticipating additional stress, I make sure that my exercise is planned in and can take out some of my frustrations on the treadmill or use yoga to reconnect with my inner self.

If things are becoming untenable in work, then it is sometimes worth considering discussing this with a line manager. Sometimes when stress takes hold, it can be hard to see the bigger picture. A discussion with a manager can help prioritise your workload and can also be used to ask for additional support when necessary.

This is the same for study. You may wish to let tutors know of your condition, as this can be helpful when you are feeling under pressure. You may be able to ask for a deadline extension or additional support. This is not an excuse for poor planning! If there in one thing you should take away from this book, it is to organise your life around bipolar disorder. The worst thing you can do is be the cause of additional and unnecessary pressure and stress. Where you have a deadline for an assignment, plan for it. Do not leave it until the last minute. If you plan your study or work in reasonable chunks, with a clear goal and commitment to a deadline, it can be of enormous help in managing your condition.

Implement Your New Knowledge

Use the tips and information from the previous chapters to start implementing your knowledge from mood diaries and triggers to a healthy inner life. All these techniques, combined with basic lifestyle changes, can help in managing your condition, preventing the severity of further episodes and more importantly, give you back some power and control.

Top Tips and Key Action Points:

- Consider changes you can make to your lifestyle. Each small thing can contribute to remaining well.
- Use a timetable to monitor your activities and demands on your time. This will help identify possible stress and allow you to put things in place.
- Learn to say no. You cannot remain well and be all things to all people at all times.
- Consider the benefits of exercise in consultation with your doctor.
- Stick to a sleep routine and practice sensible sleep hygiene.
- Look at changes you could make to your diet and also to your intake of alcohol and other stimulants.
- Consider other therapeutic activities such as massage and so on; but source your practitioners carefully.
- Consider joining a support group, especially if you feel isolated. It may not be for you, but this model does work for some.
- Consider your condition when planning your career or your work/study activities.
- Acknowledge any concerning work/study patterns and seek support where appropriate.
- If you have the choice, think about whether you wish to disclose your condition. This is a very personal decision.

CHAPTER FOURTEEN

The Spouse's Perspective

Before we get to the conclusion of the book, I asked my husband Steven to write a few words about his journey with bipolar disorder. I would encourage you to share this chapter with your partner and any other significant people. Here are Steven's thoughts:

I can be strong; I can be vulnerable, and somewhere in between. I can be loud; I can be quiet, and somewhere in between. I can be cynical; I can be idealistic, and somewhere in between. I don't have bipolar disorder, but I live with it. The author of this book, my wife Wendy, asked me to write a few words to contribute. My brief, simply, was to write about what I have learned with respect to bipolar disorder, and more specifically, my thoughts and observations as a partner and husband to somebody who has the condition. I have learned about myself in this relationship and, more specifically, have learned how to work together with my wife as much as possible to manage the condition, as opposed to it managing us.

The first thing to point out is that from the very beginning, Wendy was open about having bipolar disorder. This was her decision, which she didn't take lightly, but as we were colleagues working closely together on a project, she felt that it was the right thing to do and only fair. I hadn't heard the term "bipolar disorder" at the time. Wendy explained that it was previously referred to as "manic depression". I then felt I had more of an understanding. I was wrong.

Having studied, at varying levels, youth and community studies and counselling and worked in a "caring profession", I felt confident at the time in my ability not to judge and to empathise. Refusing to be judgmental was easy. I didn't know enough about the condition to have an opinion. The empathy, however, was much more difficult. Don't get me wrong – the intent to empathise was there, it was the insight that was missing.

I know that if you're the spouse, partner, parent, sibling, friend, or colleague of somebody with bipolar disorder, then by reading this book, you are already doing more to learn about the condition than I initially did. Looking back, the more I grew to know Wendy, and the closer we became, the more literature I would read to try to gain a greater understanding of Wendy's condition. As somebody writing in a book about bipolar disorder, it would be counter-intuitive of me to suggest that you don't try to learn about the condition. Just don't try to be an expert on it. It is more advisable, perhaps, to be more of an expert on the person with bipolar disorder than the condition itself. In particular, learn about those potential triggers that can cause episodes for the person in question and how to avoid them where possible. This is easier said than done, and in my case, I am still learning.

Thinking back to the first episode that Wendy had when we were together, I felt so helpless, uninformed and scared. Keeping an open and honest dialogue ever since has helped us both greatly in working together in combating the condition. As a husband, I can't stress enough the benefit of practising this high level of communication. This goes for any sufferer and their primary carer. Not speaking about the condition, its triggers and consequences isn't an option, as far as I have experienced – ignoring it won't make it go away.

Indeed, as Wendy will have covered elsewhere in the book, it is much better to embrace the situation you are in. As somebody who doesn't have bipolar disorder, I have still embraced it and taken a sense of ownership of it. In a sense, I have married it. I will never define Wendy by her condition (and she will never let me!) However, there is no getting away from the condition and it is always there – in good times and bad. The key is to accept this and work with it. Better to learn how to live with it, and treat it with the respect it deserves. Wendy will have covered many tips and techniques on self-management, and some of these will have covered lifestyle choices and managing potential triggers.

For example, there have times when we have planned to go to a social event and Wendy has had to cancel in order to best maintain her mental well-being. Early in our relationship, this could be frustrating – I still had some learning to do. It is necessary to be mindful of the important things in life – yes, seeing family and friends at social events is important, as it helps to maintain relationships. However, is dutifully carrying on and going to the event, when the sufferer is feeling vulnerable, really worth the potential consequences?

There is a temptation to attend the planned event anyway, to ensure that you don't feel like you are disappointing people or letting them down. What you need to remember is that it will be much quicker for those people to recover from said disappointment than it will be for the sufferer to recover from putting themselves under too much pressure or stress. Quite simply, it is a question of prioritising. There are always choices to make, but think of the repercussions of your decisions. This may seem like a rather negative viewpoint, but it is actually positive in that you are giving the illness the respect it deserves. Moreover, it is a necessary way of managing the condition and maintaining some control.

This book contains some excellent tips and action points on a wide variety of things that will be beneficial to people with bipolar disorder. In a nutshell, these are fundamentally about self-management. When I set about writing this entry, it was with the intention of possibly sharing a key piece of advice or insight as to how to work with your partner who has the condition – from one person without bipolar disorder to another. However, as I write, the main concept I would like to get across to whoever is reading is this: the key to living healthily and successfully with bipolar disorder starts with the person with the illness.

Wendy has often mentioned how supportive I have been over the years and, as much as I try and as much as I give in terms of support and strength, I can only do so due to

*the amount of self-management she undertakes. Wendy
will thank me for being there through difficult times,
for making sacrifices, for not laying blame and for
understanding. However, I honestly wonder how much
I would be able to do this continually if Wendy was not
as responsible in her self-care and management as she is.
Wendy may thank me for the love and support I give her,
but it is fair to say that I am thankful and grateful to
her for allowing me the opportunity to do so. In all
marriages, each partner should be on an equal footing to
the other. It would be remiss of me not to point out also
that she is my strength, my inspiration, and I would be
lost without her. Bipolar disorder is a huge part of our
life together, but so are laughter, joy and hope.*

*For those of you reading this book, whether you have
bipolar disorder or not, I hope you are able to gain
greater clarity, understanding and knowledge of how to
deal with and live with the condition. It is due to
Wendy's dedication to staying well, accepting her
condition and making the most of life that the writing of
this book has been possible and with it, hopefully, for
you to become your bipolar life coach.*

Conclusion

I am confident that you can improve your life if you are living with bipolar disorder. It may be in the smallest of ways or it may mean completely reshaping your relationship with the condition. Whether you use all the chapters in the book or just take some basic tips, I am hopeful that by becoming your own bipolar life coach, you will gain a greater respect for bipolar disorder. You may be able to shift some of the power back in your favour, by being able to better manage your condition and getting some control back.

A diagnosis of bipolar disorder can be terrifying, but it need not be a death sentence. I am proof that if you respect it, gain insight, change your thought processes and put things in place to manage it, you *can* live with it. It will not be easy and it will get ugly. There will be days when you think you just can't go on. I have had days in the past where I looked out at the future and felt with every fibre of my being that I just couldn't do it anymore. I could not take another day living with this, but I did and I do.

I know the damage another episode can bring. I know it can negatively influence your relationships, your work and your overall well-being. I will not pretend otherwise. But this is one thing in life that you cannot get out of. You cannot make it go away, and you should ignore it at your peril. No matter how much you hate it right now or during an episode, you do have to accept it; you need to make peace with it and to work on a healthy relationship with it. I do not know that there is any other option.

There may well be times in the future when many of us experience a severe episode once again. I am sure that, like me, this fills you with dread. It is a terrifying thought. We should also accept it and strive each and every day to do all we can to reduce the likelihood of it.

I have met many people through my work with many conditions and with traumatic pasts. I am often thankful that *all* I have is bipolar disorder. These are the cards we have been dealt, and we must play our hand well.

If it were not for bipolar disorder, I would have not been to the places in my mind and my moods that I have. There is beauty in my condition. I have seen such darkness and such light that, when well, it gives me a unique perspective on life. It makes me appreciate the good times all the more. There have been times when I almost didn't make it. What a gift that I am here to experience today. It has allowed me to truly connect with myself and reach an inner life that many do not have. Granted, I was forced into self-reflection, but I am healthier and happier for it. Having bipolar disorder has allowed me to see the love and kindness that others have the capacity to give. I am so very fortunate to have been able to experience this.

Now it's over to you. You have bipolar disorder. You are you and you are unique – go forward safe in the knowledge that this is just fine. Be a trailblazer, be a role model, be positive and be well. I wish you courage, strength and love.

References

1 *The Secret Life of the Manic Depressive. BBC2. First aired 19ᵗʰ September 2006*

2 *Redfield Jamison, K. (1997) An Unquiet Mind: A Memoir of Moods and Madness. Picador, London*

3 *Bipolar Disorder Factsheet. Rethink Mental Illness. www.rethink.org Jan 2012*

4 *http://www. nhs. uk/Conditions/Counselling/Pages/ Talking-therapies. aspxhttp://www. nhs. uk/Conditions/ Counselling/Pages/Talking-therapies. aspx May 2012*